Strategic Concepts

CLIVE SUTTON

MACMILLAN
Business

First published 1998 by
MACMILLAN PRESS LTD
Houndmills, Basingstoke, Hampshire RG21 6XS
and London
Companies and representatives
throughout the world

ISBN 0–333–72529–8 hardcover
ISBN 0–333–72530–1 paperback

A catalogue record for this book is available from the British Library.

10   9   8   7   6   5   4   3   2   1
07   06   05   04   03   02   01   00   99   98

Copy-edited and typeset by Povey–Edmondson
Tavistock and Rochdale, England

Printed in Great Britain by
Antony Rowe Ltd
Chippenham, Wiltshire

Contents

List of Figures

Preface

Contemporary corporate strategy has seen a plethora of instant solutions such as re-engineering, outsourcing or continuous innovation, and earlier strategies based on scale or scope have been rejected in favour of a clear focus on core activities. This book attempts to present a balance which sets these strategic trends in their historical context and assesses their current relevance. After a general introduction it considers size (re-engineering), integration (outsourcing), diversification (focus), innovation (continuous and discontinuous) and mergers, together with divestment and strategic alliances. In each case the topics are considered as a series of options and not as strategic imperatives.

The book therefore focuses on broad notions of strategy and on strategic thinking. It is a book about thinking rather than doing – although I dare to hope that practitioners may still find something here to interest them. It is intended primarily as a textbook for undergraduate programmes in Business Studies or Business Administration, which universally include course units in Business Strategy as a unifying or contextual theme, and it should also serve as an introductory text for those students at Diploma or Masters level in Business Administration whose earlier qualifications and experience come from a different discipline.

It is written from an Economics perspective and draws on notions of opportunity costs, resources, transactions and competition as sources of inspiration for strategic thought, in a world of uncertainty in which our attempts to behave rationally are bounded by our limited understanding. But this is not an Economics textbook and it does not assume any prior knowledge of Economic Theory. A nodding acquaintance might help with some passages but it is never essential.

I believe that every student of business, and indeed everyone who works in business, needs to know what strategy is and why it is important. They need to understand what their organisation is trying to do, and why. They may not be strategists but, if their organisation has any pretensions to good management, they should be prepared to contribute ideas to the formulation of strategy. That belief determines the focus of this book, but there are two things which the book does not try to do. It is not concerned with the implementation of strategy and it does not go into any detail on technical subjects like Business Finance. These topics are important – many good strategies will fail if they are not properly implemented, and Business Finance is an essential component of the higher strategist's art. But logically these topics come after the groundwork of a general understanding has been laid. Push them too soon, and the ultimate objectives may be lost in a welter of technical detail.

The book therefore aims to encourage thinking before application, and the examples look for lessons which can be applied as readily in a global setting as they can within specific national boundaries. Many of the topics are as applicable to not-for-profit organisations as they are to business enterprises. Universities, theatres, museums, charities and similar bodies all face strategic problems. Universities must position themselves in relation to other educational institutions and research bodies; theatres and museums must determine their focus and the extent of any collaboration with others; and charities must understand the logic of their target market. But the problem with not-for-profit organisations is that so much of their experience is *sui generis*. A depth of local knowledge is needed before the strategic choices can be understood, and one can never be certain without further detailed knowledge that any lessons can be applied in a different context. By contrast, the spread of global competition, although incomplete, has generally served to ensure that business experience transcends national and cultural boundaries. Hence, although the analysis in this book is broadly applicable to all strategic decisions, the examples have been taken only from business and commerce in order to ensure that they are as generalisable as possible.

Many of these examples come from books or articles, or from unascribed reports in periodicals like *The Economist*, or from company reports. These sources are acknowledged in the text. Other examples have been put together from a variety of different sources and in these cases no specific references can be given. For all these examples, I acknowledge my debt to the named or anonymous writers on whose work I have drawn. Further, in a few cases the published information has been supplemented by additional information provided by the companies concerned, and in these cases – especially BAA, Manx Airlines, Peptide Therapeutics and Thermo Electron – I am particularly grateful to the organisations and to the individuals concerned for their help, although of course any errors or omissions in the text are entirely of my own making.

Thanks are also due to the staff of the Isle of Man College Library, and especially to Tim Kenyon, for patient and unfailing support for my efforts to trace references through the British Lending Library.

Among the many colleagues and students who have influenced my own strategic thinking there are two who deserve special mention. I must record special thanks to Peter Jackson who first suggested that this might be worth doing, and to my wife Dorothy whose patience helped to ensure that it could be done.

CLIVE SUTTON

1 The Nature of Strategic Thinking

INTRODUCTION

What is strategy? Why is it important?

Dictionaries usually look at military applications to define the origins of the word. Strategy is then concerned with larger movements such as the operation of a campaign, and distinguished from tactics which relate to the conduct of a particular battle, or detailed actions which arise as a consequence of strategic decisions. Business strategy retains the same broad meaning. It is concerned with the general disposition of business rather than day-to-day operations. But the distinction between business strategy and tactics is less well defined, and discussions of business strategy will sometimes include tactics under the heading of strategic implementation.

This book focuses on the disposition of the business and its resources. It is concerned with the issues of the campaign rather than the detail of individual battles. A recent example may help to illustrate this focus and to explain the importance of strategic decisions in business, before we try to pick out the definitions in more detail.

An Example: The Daimler-Benz Group

The Daimler-Benz Group is one of Germany's largest manufacturing organisations, with assets of more than DM90 billion, covering cars and vehicles, aerospace, general engineering and commercial services such as insurance brokerage and real estate management. Between 1986 and 1991 its net income remained fairly stable at around DM1.8 billion. After 1991 it fell more or less continuously to a net loss in 1995 of DM5.7 billion, or 5.5 per cent of the Group's revenue. By 1997, however, the Group could announce that it had returned to the black for fiscal year 1996, with consolidated net income of DM2.8 billion.

What caused these changes in the Group's fortunes? There is, of course, no single explanation. It is true that some two-thirds of the loss in 1995 was ascribed to 'extraordinary results', which included non-recurring expenses. The results in 1996 were also aided by the depreciation of the D-mark and by a modest economic recovery, but these are essentially transient factors which cannot explain a longer-term trend. A major part of the turnaround, and any prospect of sustainable gains, must be ascribed to a significant change in the company's strategy.

1

During the 1980s the Group had spread its activities more and more widely, like a lot of other companies. It was rich in cash and eager to grow, and it bought its way into a number of unfamiliar businesses. In practice, it lacked the breadth of expertise needed to run these effectively, and as a result its net income rose by less than 10 per cent between 1986 and 1991 while consolidated revenues rose by 45 per cent.

After a peak in 1991, Daimler-Benz's net income declined steadily. In response, the Group shed nearly 20 per cent of its work force between 1991 and 1995; it reversed an earlier policy of acquisitive expansion by disposing of its domestic appliances division in 1994; and then in 1995 it undertook a systematic review of each corporate unit. This review included an assessment of the market and of market competition, estimates of future income and of the capital requirements for each activity, and an assessment of risk. At the same time the company changed its management procedures to set tougher financial targets for each unit, with less direct intervention from corporate headquarters. -

The review had relatively little impact on the Mercedes-Benz unit, which produces the well-known cars and commercial vehicles, although there had already been some significant changes in the way in which the unit was run. Most of the impact of the review fell on two loss-making corporate units: AEG Daimler-Benz Industrie (AEG), the Engineering unit, and Daimler-Benz Aerospace (DASA). Within AEG, resources were to be concentrated on rail systems, microelectronics, diesel engines and postal automation equipment, while the Group's previous interests in energy systems and automation were sold off to other companies. Within DASA, the main change was the withdrawal of support for Fokker, the Dutch manufacturer of regional aircraft, although DASA also sold Telefunken Sendertechnik in 1995 and gave up its majority stake in Dornier Medizintechnik in 1996. Commenting on the outcome of the review, Hilmar Kopper, the Chairman of the Supervisory Board of Daimler-Benz, claimed that 'The Board of Management has decisively begun the elimination of weak points in the group portfolio. With its strategic plans, the Board has laid a strong foundation for the future development of the group' (Annual Report 1995, p. 71).

Clearly the changes in the Group's fortunes accompanied changes in its strategy. Other factors influenced the outcome, but there is a strong presumption that the changes in strategy had a major impact on the Group's performance.

STRATEGY, CHOICE AND UNCERTAINTY

The example of Daimler-Benz does not cover all aspects of strategy, but it does give a starting point for further discussion. Note that in the example, the Group's review was triggered by the relative stagnation and decline in its fortunes. However, the aim of the review was not simply to reverse the immediate decline but to ensure that the Group was soundly based for future development. Strategic thinking like this involves an attempt to find a special position in the market which best suits the firm's skills and resources. It has to deal with the fundamental nature of the firm, and how its resources can best be deployed to meet its objectives. In effect, it is an attempt to define what it is that makes this firm different from any other.

This emphasis on being different is important. In quantum mechanics the Pauli Principle of Exclusion holds that no two particles can exist in identical quantum states, and substantially the same principle holds true in strategic space. No two firms can be identical. Further, if two firms are very similar it would never be possible for one to gain ascendancy over the other. Conversely, if a firm is to gain a strategic advantage it must seek to identify and exploit the characteristics which make it unique, provided that this can be done in ways which attract customers and do not alienate suppliers.

Strategic Choice

When it undertakes a strategic review a firm may find that its position in one market is too weak, or may need too great a commitment of resources to make it viable, and it must then change the scope of its activities to focus on the market opportunities which it can exploit successfully with its limited resources. In other cases a firm may seek to strengthen its competitive position by increasing or changing the nature of its commitment. It may anticipate a change in the nature of its markets or even anticipate the emergence of a completely new market, and then try to ensure that it has the skills and the position to take advantage of the changes, or even to influence the nature of the changes as they occur.

All such cases involve choices. No one can respond to every opportunity which comes along, and the choice of strategy, while it tries to find the best stance for one set of opportunities, will inevitably close off others which are believed to be inferior in some way. These unwanted alternatives may seem to be very attractive to another firm with a different set of resources, but this is irrelevant. Each firm must determine its own strategy in relation to its own skills and perceptions, and these may be very different from those of other firms: as we saw in the example of Daimler-Benz, some activities which had ceased to be attractive within the Group were readily sold to other firms which presumably had good reason to expect that their acquisitions would be profitable. In some cases it may seem to be sensible for a firm to hold on to markets it does not want if it believes that they might otherwise help to reinforce the position of actual or potential competitors, but this can still be a dangerous argument, especially if competitors can find other ways to strengthen their position while the firm in question is left holding on to activities which undermine its total performance.

Uncertainty

Some strategic decisions may be implemented fairly quickly, as an unwanted unit may be sold if there is a willing buyer. Others may take longer, as when new skills and new contacts have to be built up for a developing market. But all are concerned to position the organisation for operations in the future, and are therefore affected by uncertainty, because the future can never be known until it is here. This may affect strategy in three ways, which we might refer to as 'position', 'routine' and 'influence'.

Position

First, position. The strategy may be seen as an attempt to contain uncertainty and make it easier to live with. For example, most of us know that we can handle a problem more easily when we are on our home ground than we can when we are in a foreign country, especially if it is a country which we have not visited before and where we do not know the local language and customs. And so we take precautions when we go to strange places. We carry extra medicines, we travel with a friend who has been there before, or in extreme cases we may call the whole thing off and go to somewhere familiar where we feel more comfortable. In the same way a firm may respond to uncertainty by building reserves, forming alliances with other firms or excluding some types of business from its portfolio.

Routine

Secondly, routine. The decision to exclude some types of business may be reinforced by the adoption of set routines and procedures for taking decisions. It is often argued that when uncertainty makes it difficult to identify the preferred pattern of behaviour, individuals or organisations will adopt mechanisms which automatically shut out some possible choices and limit the range of information which is used for making decisions (see, for example, Heine, 1983). As part of this process, strategic decisions may consciously restrict the range of options from which future choices may be made. But there is a danger. Most rules are either based on precedent, and so assume continuity, or they are derived from formulae which assume that behaviour can be modelled in predictable ways. Either may help an organisation to come to terms with uncertainty, but they become harmful if they are retained as conditions change and the underlying logic loses its validity.

Influence

The third response to uncertainty may be a search for greater influence if a firm believes that its current actions may help to give it more control over future events. Consider, for example, the future state of the market in which the firm operates. No firm can know with complete certainty how the market will develop, because that will depend not only upon the firm's own actions, but also upon the actions of customers and competitors as well as other extraneous events. Nevertheless the future market in (say) five or ten years' time will not appear suddenly like Venus arising from the waves, but must depend in some degree upon the events in the intervening years. A firm's current strategy on things like mergers or new product development or integration may be expected to influence the market's development and so make the current uncertainty more bearable.

OBJECTIVES

Some firms tend to equate strategy with 'the way we do things'. This may be helpful, in so far as 'the way we do things' says something about the firm's stance in the market place. But it can be misleading. Strategy is concerned primarily with what is done rather than how it is done. It may be more constructive to think of strategy as 'doing the right things', in contrast to operations ('doing things right') or administration ('organising things the right way').

Nevertheless, once we are aware of the potential confusion, 'the way we do things' may help to put the firm in perspective. It defines the way the firm likes to be seen, and can say quite a lot about what the firm is trying to achieve, its objectives. Unfortunately, the term 'objective' may also be a source of confusion, and it has prompted much discussion in the literature. There are many apparent synonyms – objectives, goals, targets, mission, aims, and so on – and each may have its own shade of distinction. Analysts may ask: whose objectives? where do they come from? how are they measured? are they followed consistently or intermittently? For our purpose, however, we may focus on four issues which have a particular bearing on strategy. These are the time horizon, the nature of a firm's objectives, the use of proxy objectives and the problem of multiple objectives.

The Time Horizon

Objectives have a time dimension. Some are short-term and short-lived, whereas others relate to a more distant future and are more or less permanent. The short-term ones are often dominated by the longer-term ones, and may be seen as steps on the way towards a future objective. The most distant objectives are usually identified in the firm's mission, which has much in common with a vocation for an individual, and may be just a statement of intent with few if any precise measures of achievement. At the other extreme we have targets, which are precise steps to be achieved within a precise time frame. In between, for a longer but more variable time horizon, we have goals. These may be specified as discrete acts: 'Acquire a distributor in market X', say, or 'Establish sales outlets in country A with target sales of B by end of first year'. Alternatively the goals may be specified in quantitative terms such as market share or sales volume, but are less precise than targets and may sometimes be considered as an average value or range to define the acceptable limits of performance.

These definitions are rarely followed very carefully in general discussion, and it may often be difficult to decide which is intended in a particular context. Generally this does not matter very much and it is more important to recognise the differences than it is to try to force particular cases to match a particular definition.

A simple, personal illustration may help to clarify the differences. Suppose that you have just joined an international relief agency and are on your way to Africa to work on famine relief. As you leave home with your suitcase to catch a train to the airport, a neighbour asks you where you are going. You might say 'I'm on my way to the station', or 'I'm off to Africa', or 'I'm going to help with famine relief'. These statements correspond broadly with the definitions of target, goal and mission. Each may be the correct answer in the appropriate context, but not in all contexts. Only the first would be of much use if the neighbour offered you a lift, but it is the mission statement which says most about what makes your journey different from anybody else's.

Clearly it is the mission statement which is most closely related to strategy, but it is also the least precise. There is therefore a danger that the lack of precision means a vagueness which makes it impossible to judge whether or not the objective has ever been achieved. If the mission is not precise, any outcome may be made to seem consistent with the mission, just as many politicians will claim after five years in office that whatever has happened was intended in their election manifestos. Hence we have intermediate goals to define measurable steps which contribute towards the mission. But if these are applied too rigorously, we may have the countervailing problem which arises when short or medium-term objectives are followed without adequate consideration of their long-term implications, and so are allowed to distort and dominate the mission. There can be no perfect solution in an uncertain world. The balance is a matter of judgement, which may be rare but remains as one of the essential attributes of senior management.

The Nature of a Firm's Objectives

What is a firm? It is a definable legal entity but it has no mind of its own. Ultimately it acquires its character from the individuals who are associated with it. They may learn to work as a team and the team may generate characteristics which distinguish it from other teams and which persist as some of the members of the team change, but it is still dependent on the members of the team to give it its character. Similarly, the objectives of the firm will be set by individuals, and may vary as the individuals vary.

Of course, individual discretion will be constrained to a greater or lesser degree. Highly competitive markets will reduce the degree of freedom faced by those who run the firm, and in all market conditions firms will be constrained to obey the law and may feel themselves to be constrained to accept political pressures from other members of the community with specific interests in civil liberties or environmental protection.

Within the firm, the major objectives are those set by senior management, and 'the objectives of the firm' are most commonly defined in this way. The managers will have their own objectives which may influence the way they choose to lead the firm and there is always the chance that this will lead to idiosyncratic behaviour. In practice, however, it will be true that most managers will have chosen business as the appropriate arena in which to pursue their objectives rather than (say) the church or politics or social services, and so it is not unreasonable to assume that the objectives of most managers will be broadly consistent with what is loosely termed the 'business ethic', and will emphasise the profitability, size and growth of their firm.

Further, in setting their own objectives, managers must be aware of at least four other groups who hold some stake in the firm and are concerned with the outcome of its activities. These include the shareholders (who will generally be looking for some combination of income, capital growth and security), customers (who seek value for money, but may also develop some moral judgements about the firms they wish to buy from), employees (with concerns about fair pay, conditions of service and job security), and suppliers (who expect fair prices and terms of business). They will all have varying degrees of influence over the management and, hence, over the objectives of the firm. Some will be transient stakeholders while others will look for a more permanent relationship. The more permanent stakeholders are likely to be more concerned with the firm's strategic thinking, and they may tolerate a minor tactical blunder or a misplaced target so long as they continue to be satisfied that the strategy is sound and that the firm is broadly on line to achieve its goals and/or its mission. This tolerance may also be conditioned by social and cultural factors. For example, Lasserre and Schütte (1995) suggest that in Japan the potential conflict between

employees and other stakeholders has been reduced by the employees' desire
to identify with a group rather than striving for individual achievement, as
well as by the implicit contracts which in the past have offered lifelong
employment for lifelong loyalty.

Objectives and Proxies

Some measures which appear as goals or targets may not be objectives in
their own right but may be chosen as indicators, because they are believed to
be associated with true objectives. For example, this may be true on
occasions of market share which may be chosen as a goal only because it
is assumed that a significant increase in market share will lead to higher and/
or more stable profits, and not because a large or small market share is of
any particular interest on its own.

Instrumental or proxy goals of this nature may be based on personal
experience or they may be suggested by examination of other firms. For
some years guidelines of this nature have been made available to subscribers
to the Profit Impact of Marketing Strategy (PIMS) data base. Starting from
an initiative by the US General Electric Company, the data base started in
1973 with 57 major corporations which provided financial and other
information on 620 business units for the years 1970–2. It is now held by
the Strategic Planning Institute of Boston, Massachusetts, and covers over
3,000 units. Detailed data are available only to subscribing companies, but
analyses of the data have been published from time to time following the
initial analysis in Buzzel, Gale and Sultan (1975). The main results have
suggested that profitability may be adversely affected by an increase in
capital intensity but promoted by improvements in product or service
quality or by increases in market share relative to those of competitors.

Proxy goals of this sort may be used for several reasons. It may be that
some true objectives can only be assessed after the event and/or they may be
subject to wide margins of error and/or they may be rather abstract concepts
which do not immediately suggest how they might be achieved. This may be
particularly true of financial objectives. For example, profits can only be
calculated as a residual, and forecasts are therefore less accurate than the
estimates of sales and costs from which they are derived. By contrast, sales
revenue and market share are more predictable and may also appear to give
a more immediate indication of the kinds of policy which might make them
achievable.

Multiple Objectives

'Saki' (the short-story writer, H. H. Munro) once suggested that people who
have immense wealth have no need to look for titles or honours or dignities

because these things will come to them automatically as a consequence of their wealth. Economists often take a similar view of profits and assume that a single objective of profit maximisation will encompass or dominate all others. This is convenient for model building, which needs a precise objective if it is to produce clear solutions, and in this context the assumption of profit maximisation has allowed many elegant models which produce clear generalisations about the behaviour of firms. But individual firms may not conform to the general model, and when we come to deal with individual firms we may find that they are less single-minded and less consistent than would be required for a predictive model. They may have a number of medium-term goals which may include some or all of profits, capital growth, return on shareholders' equity, stock market valuation, sales revenue, market share, innovation and global market penetration. Even if some of these are only proxy objectives, they are still part of the firm's decision-making processes and there may be no clear formula for specifying a trade-off when the objectives come into conflict with one another, as, for example, when increased sales revenue can only be achieved at the expense of profits.

How can firms live with such inconsistencies? First we may note that the inconsistencies are more likely to arise between goals or targets than they are within the mission. The relative precision of goals and targets may highlight the conflicts from time to time but the more abstract mission statements are less likely to do so. When there are inconsistencies at any level, the most likely alternatives to a full trade-off will involve either or both satisficing and ranking.

First, a firm may specify a series of numerical goals to satisfy its multiple objectives, which might be expressed in the form 'x per cent return on shareholders' equity, y per cent share in each key market and z per cent per annum sales growth'. Such goals may be set from an extrapolation of past performance, modified to allow for changes in external conditions, or by benchmarking against competitors, or by some combination of the two. For example, the Swedish vehicle manufacturer, Volvo, set its objective for return on shareholders' equity in December 1995 as 'to achieve a return of 12 to 15 % on shareholders' equity, based upon current levels of interest rates, over an economic cycle, which would exceed the current average for the industry' (Annual Report, 1995, p. 6)

These numerical goals are not set at the maximum levels which might be achieved, but at levels which are believed to be satisfactory for all concerned – hence 'satisficing'. Multiple goals which are set in this way may be mutually consistent without the need for a trade-off if they are set at a level which is high enough to be satisfactory but is still below the maximum which might be achieved for each goal in isolation. On the other hand, more ambitious goals, or a deterioration in the environment which makes the goals harder to achieve, may force managers to choose between them. This may happen, for example, if it becomes clear that a sales goal can be achieved only by accepting a cut in prices and profits.

If adverse conditions make it impossible to achieve all goals simultaneously, the alternative may be to accept an explicit or implicit ranking of goals. The ranking would be implicit if one goal was simply ignored while others were pursued. It would become explicit if the goals were recast in the form 'increase sales by x per cent per annum, subject to profits not less than y per cent'. It is then clear that the profit goal is paramount if any attempt to increase sales would force profits below y per cent in the short term, but those who favour a sales goal would be free to pursue their objective as soon as economic conditions allow.

STRATEGIC ANALYSIS

The discussion so far indicates that strategic choices must be directed to achieving the firm's mission in a distant and uncertain future, along a route which may be defined by a series of medium-term goals. To this we may now add that strategic choices must seek to achieve a favourable balance between the firm's capability and the opportunities which it faces. The process is characterised in Figure 1.1.

This model serves to emphasise the interaction between the characteristics of the firm and the context or environment in which it operates. Sensible choices must be made within the area where the characteristics and context overlap, or are clearly consistent with each other. But the model also emphasises that the choices may change the context or the characteristics in some way and so expand or contract the area of overlap. A firm's choices will determine its conduct, or strategic actions, which in turn feed back to have some effect on the future characteristics of the firm and its environment. This must therefore be seen as an iterative process rather than a single decision. There may be only a few iterations if the context is stable and the outcomes are expected to be favourable, but frequent reappraisal may be

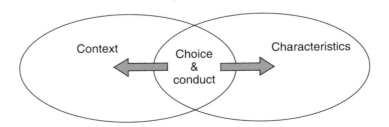

Figure 1.1   *The focus for strategic analysis*

needed if the context is unstable and/or if the outcomes are highly uncertain or certainly unattractive.

Characteristics

The characteristics define the firm as a collection of interdependent resources – capital assets, employees, skills, experience, contacts and image – together with its mission and general objectives. The important resources are not transient items like advertising or research expenditure but the assets or stocks of resource – the brand name or innovative skill – which have been created by these flows of money. Similarly for employees the essential characteristic is not simply the number employed but the skills and experience which have been embodied in groups or teams of employees and which cannot be replicated at short notice.

Two points must be remembered in any attempt to assess the characteristics of a firm. The first is that all values are relative. The second is that no values are immutable. These may be considered in turn.

Relative Assessments

The purpose of any assessment is not simply to define the firm's resources, but to appraise them. We need to know how good they are, and this can be done only if we have some measure of quality. Given that the firm is competing to survive and grow in particular markets the only relevant measure of quality is a competitive one. Resources must be appraised in relation to those of competitors and in terms of their relevance for the markets concerned. We all know that in the kingdom of the blind, the one-eyed man is king; but it may equally be true that two good eyes are inadequate if everyone else has a pair of binoculars.

The first essential is therefore to establish the key factors which are required for success in each market. The second is to assess one firm's ability to meet these factors relative to the abilities of its most successful competitors. This must be done critically: there is a very real and natural danger of overestimating the importance of the things we do well while turning a blind eye to our weaknesses. It must also be done, so far as is possible, using assessments which can be supported by hard facts: it may not be very meaningful to be told that one firm is more innovative than another unless it can be established (say) that it has consistently introduced a greater number of successful new products.

The assessment must be done separately for each market, because the key success factors and the relevant competitors may be different in each market. From the firm's point of view the most convenient basis for this appraisal may be its existing administrative units (divisions, departments, and so on), but this may need to be reconsidered if the divisions cut across market boundaries. Note also that the emphasis on relevant resources increases the likelihood of iteration because the definition of what resources are relevant both determines and is determined by the choices which are made.

Changing Assessments

The review must start with the firm as it is, but it may well suggest that some of the characteristics should be changed, in so far as this is possible.

For example the review may identify resources which are under-exploited in their present use. These could be disposed of, but might sometimes be used as a basis for expansion into different areas of activity, provided that they are clearly important for the new areas and also provided that the other resources needed in these new areas can be made available in the right quality at reasonable cost (for more detail see Chapter 5 below). Alternatively the review may identify areas of actual or potential weakness where the firm has resources which are inferior to those of its competitors, or lacks some of the resources needed for anticipated new market opportunities. It must then ask whether these resources can be improved or acquired at reasonable cost within a reasonable period of time, whether by purchase or training, merger or collaboration with other firms. These possibilities and their limitations are considered more fully in Chapters 5 and 7 below, but we must emphasise immediately that the relevant costs are not cash outlays but opportunity costs: the firm must ask not only whether the resources can be made available, but also whether this is the best use of the effort, skill, and money which will be needed to provide them. Often the answer will be 'no', and a graceful withdrawal will then be preferable to a rash over-commitment. Nevertheless we must recognise that strategies should be concerned with the accumulation of resources over time, and not merely with the disposition of existing resources.

Context

The previous section emphasised that resources must be appraised against relevant criteria which are appropriate for the context. But the context must also be appraised on its own, and again we must emphasise that the appraisal is not just a description, but is done to identify and assess the key features. These may well vary with each case, but we can identify three general perspectives.

First there is what Karlof (1989) describes as the 'trade logic' for each area of business: that is, the essential elements which must be understood if the firm is to have any chance of success. This may involve a very complex pattern, but the pattern is likely to include the structure of needs which generates demand, the rational and irrational factors which define product quality, the identity and likely behaviour of competitors, barriers to entry and exit, the characteristics of different channels of distribution, and the skills and technologies which are essential for the production of products or for the provision of services.

The second perspective follows immediately from the first: firms must not only know their current 'trade logic' but they must also try to anticipate changes. Firms will need some assessment of the effects of macro-economic and political changes if they are to remain ahead of their competitors, and above all they need to anticipate changes in the key success factors caused, for example, by progressive changes in the strength of competitors or in the buying habits of consumers. They must also be on the lookout for new opportunities – emerging gaps in the market which have not yet been covered by existing suppliers. Most firms will assume that they know their own markets, but industrial and commercial graveyards are full of firms which failed to recognise change until it was too late and then went down with all hands while they were still trying to respond to yesterday's problems.

The third perspective involves a consideration of long-run trends in order to anticipate areas of potential future opportunity. Under normal circumstances both the first and the second perspectives may be covered by regular monitoring, but this third perspective involves occasional intensive analyses to identify broad changes in technology or society from which future opportunities may be created. It has been described as a process of competition in which firms seek to transform industry boundaries (Hamel and Prahalad, 1994, p. 45), and it serves to emphasise that one possible reaction to any constraint is to seek to remove it, provided only that you have the power to do so. A clear insight from this perspective does not involve simply the appraisal of existing markets, but a view of future markets in which the rules of the game may be set by those firms which have the foresight and commitment to act before the market has developed and before the 'trade logic' has been defined.

Choice

The choices which make up the strategy of a firm will depend on the appraisal of strengths and weaknesses which describe its characteristics, and on the opportunities and threats which are revealed by the contextual analysis. Although it may seem to be obvious, it must be emphasised that the choices come after the appraisals: whatever may happen in politics, in business there is little value in appraisals which are undertaken solely to justify choices which have already been made. The choices must be directed to achieving the firm's objectives and must ensure that the courses of action are feasible and properly exploit the firm's resources. For the more distant future when precise outcomes are unpredictable, they must also seek to create new strengths and opportunities, and to minimise or offset threats and weaknesses.

We must also note, however, that before the choices are made there must be a range of options to choose from, and these are not given automatically by factual analyses of characteristics and context. A firm's skills, contacts and experience may be used in a variety of ways but they do not come with a handbook listing the alternative uses. Similarly, market trends may suggest areas where opportunities are to be found, but they do not define the opportunities. Those which are found will depend upon the search mechanisms which are used to complement the analyses and appraisals.

Perhaps the most common mechanism is incrementalism, as improvements are sought at the margin of existing activities. A successful development may be pushed a little bit further, or an idea which worked in one market may be tried in another. In practice, changes like these will be common, especially if experience goes unchallenged and people have no incentive to seek new solutions, or if excessive threats concentrate attention on short-term survival and drive out any deeper consideration of the longer term. The problem then is that when all firms act incrementally the likelihood is that they will all end up in more or less the same relative position as when they started. On the other hand a firm which aims to keep ahead of the pack must be able to find or create different and better opportunities than its competitors.

After the event, it is very often found that really creative strategies reflect the vision and determination of one person, or of a small group of committed individuals. Attempts to create such ideas by planning, through cross-fertilisation between groups, exposure to new stimuli, incentives which are explicitly related to innovation, and so on, carry no guarantee of success. Once again we find an area where balance, judgement and wisdom are more appropriate than standard decision rules. However it is worth repeating that the standard decisions rules are available to everyone, whereas exceptional success comes as the reward for exceptional judgement and foresight.

STRATEGIC MODES

The informal process which we have described is sometimes presented as a structured sequence of activities. For example, Howe (1986) describes the process as a sequence of six steps: setting mission and objectives; an environmental audit (opportunities and threats); an internal business audit (strengths and weaknesses); a review of opportunities to define all possible choices; a comparison of options; and a step for implementation, evaluation and control. Such a sequence may help to clarify some of the issues and so may have considerable pedagogic value, but it is simplistic and may be misleading.

We have already indicated that some parts of the appraisal must be done iteratively, which implies that there are feedback loops in the linear sequence. We have also suggested that some appraisals are normally covered by regular monitoring whereas others may require more wide-ranging investigations at less frequent intervals. It would be misleading to suggest that any decision which may have a strategic impact should only be taken after a full strategic review. After all, one of the reasons for setting a strategy is to provide a framework within which subsequent decisions can be taken. Often a strategy will persist with minor changes to reflect formal monitoring and normal business intercourse until and unless a reappraisal is indicated by a progressive decline in performance or a sudden contextual change. Mintzberg (1987a) suggests that strategies normally evolve incrementally, with occasional quantum leaps. Almost by definition we should expect that targets will change more frequently than goals, which in turn will be changed more frequently than the mission. Strategies are directed at the mission, and the main components of strategy should be equally stable, although the cumulative effect of incremental changes may eventually force a more fundamental review.

This evolution of strategy without fundamental change may take place within a continuing administrative structure. One advantage of a clear and stable strategy is that it makes for a more cohesive culture, which may be defined as the knowledge and values which can be passed on to influence behaviour. Old hands know what they are trying to achieve, and so can build informal networks or develop their own informal operating systems; newcomers know what they are signing on for and can be slotted in more readily with no sense of threat to the others. By contrast a quantum leap in strategy may require a completely new structure and culture. Fear of change will heighten uncertainty and the transition will cause insecurity for many employees, making the firm less effective while the changes are in progress. Substantial changes must therefore be managed very carefully and should not be attempted too frequently – few things are more destabilising than a management which is always pulling things up by the roots to see if they are still growing. In times of rapid environmental change and uncertainty, a key objective of senior management must be to devise a stable strategy which allows continual response to change without serious discontinuities in day-to-day operations.

We have stressed that a sound strategy is specific to the individual firm, reflecting its specific characteristics. Two firms with the same view of the environment may therefore end up with different strategies. They may also devise their strategies in different ways (see especially Mintzberg, 1987b). In smaller organisations the strategic thinking may be only semiconscious and based on the experiences of a dominant individual or small group. It will be personal, probably unarticulated and highly adaptable. By contrast many larger organisations may develop what Mintzberg refers to as an 'umbrella strategy', with a central strategy offering partial control, defining boundaries within which others may develop local strategies for operating units or divisions. We may then have a hierarchy of strategies, in which the strategy of the corporation becomes a constraint on the thinking of each business unit, which in turn helps to define the corporate strategy.

Increasingly, strategists seek to ensure that local initiatives are allowed for and incorporated into corporate strategies so that they may benefit from the widest possible corporate wisdom and ensure that the strategies are accepted and 'owned', and therefore pursued more vigorously at the local level. By contrast, tightly planned strategies which are imposed by the centre and enforced by rigid controls are less likely to generate local commitment. In general, any plan which implies a series of determinate steps leading to a unique solution must be suspect, because it assumes away the uncertainty which must be central to strategic thinking. Such plans may help to define routes towards particular goals, and may offer a series of alternative views or scenarios as an aid to strategic thinking. But they are no more than imperfect tools. Strategic thinking is ultimately concerned with the choice of what ought to be done, and where and when; it has to identify patterns in chaos and identify a need for change before the need becomes obvious. By contrast, planning is at best concerned with implementation within a given time frame and it may even be an obstacle to strategic thinking if it removes intellectual freedom. A good strategy will encourage and channel initiative. A poor plan will stifle it.

TENSIONS IN STRATEGIC THINKING

There are no perfect answers to strategic questions, nor are there any perfect formulae for solving strategic problems. Current strategic thinking involves a number of tensions which must be kept in some sort of balance. The tensions exist partly because firms must try to find a balance between alternatives and partly because different firms may make different choices and be able to sustain them either because there is no clear optimum or because competition may take a while before it undermines the less defensible choices. The alternatives may coexist within a single country. Alternatively, and perhaps more forcefully, they may coexist between different countries which retain different business cultures in spite of recent trends towards global competition.

For convenience, most of the tensions may be considered under the headings that will be used for subsequent chapters, which deal with size, supply chains, diversity, innovation and mergers, although these must be complemented by a sixth – networking – which runs through many of the others.

Size

Potential economies of scale have been confirmed in many industries, and are significant in the sense that the scale required to achieve minimum unit cost is often large in relation to the size of the industry while costs are significantly higher at smaller scales (see, for example, Pratten, 1971; Silberston, 1972; or Scherer *et al.*, 1975). But there are potential disadvantages: facilities which are appropriate for many standardised repetitive activities may be highly inflexible; repetitive work in large anonymous structures may cause boredom and hence may lead to restrictive practices; changes may be more difficult to co-ordinate and communication may be subject to more noise in larger organisations.

An effective strategy must seek to find a balance which meets the needs of the market place. The balance may also affect relationships between firms of different size and may indicate that strategic choices should be size-dependent. These issues are considered in Chapter 3.

Supply Chains

From some perspectives a single firm is only one step in a chain of interrelated organisations which deliver supplies to customers. Some chains in manufacturing and in service industries like television broadcasting may be very complex and involve many firms. Other service industries which depend on a one-to-one relationship, as in hairdressing, may have much shorter chains. Regardless of the length and complexity of the chain, each individual link is justified only if it adds value to the work of others.

Sometimes it may appear that one stage dominates the rest, in that the firms at that stage have a major co-ordinating role in the chain. This stage is generally taken as the focus for strategic analysis. However, the location of this stage within the chain may vary between industries and may change over time within the same industry. For example the initiative may sometimes be taken by retailers, sometimes by manufacturers and sometimes by suppliers. A large retail chain like Marks and Spencer may be typical of the first, motor assembly firms may exemplify the second, and the producers of crude oil illustrate the third.

Control may therefore appear to be more important from some perspectives than from others. Where it is important, it may be effected in different ways, either by integrated ownership or through looser relationships between independent firms. These issues are considered in Chapter 4.

Diversity

Diversification occurs whenever a firm combines two or more activities which are not related as stages in the supply chain, although they may use similar inputs or be sold through similar outlets. Diversified firms therefore offer more than one product line or type of service, but most firms are probably diversified to some degree and our interest is in the degree rather than the fact of diversification. An increase in the degree may be beneficial, offering opportunities for economies of scope, which are defined as existing whenever it is cheaper to provide different items through a single organisation than through separate organisations. Economies of scope may be found in production if two or more distinct products can share a common process, but they appear to be more important for support activities like research or distribution or finance when increases in the number of products will increase the aggregate requirement and may therefore allow economies of scale to be realised in each separate activity.

On the other hand diversification also makes management more complex and the overall efficiency of the firm may then suffer as a result. Some recent changes in Europe and America might seem to indicate that these disadvantages are becoming increasingly important. For example, firms like Daimler-Benz have off-loaded some activities (see page 2 above) while conglomerates like Beatrice and Hanson have been broken up. But there are other features: apparent conglomerates like Virgin or KKR persist; some industries are becoming more diversified as the barriers which once divided markets become less significant, as in the UK financial sector with the increasing overlap between banks, building societies and insurance companies; and diversification generally remains stronger in Asia Pacific, for example among the South Korean *chaebol* or conglomerates run by the Overseas Chinese.

Some of these variations reflect differences in culture, but most reflect the balance of interest for individual firms. The nature of the balance will be considered in Chapter 5.

Innovation

Innovation involves the adoption of procedures or products which are perceived as being new by the adopter. From the perspective of an individual firm, it involves new ways of doing things and/or new products or services offered to customers. Whether or not some other firms have already made similar innovations is irrelevant for this definition, although it may have a crucial effect on the outcome – it may or not pay to be first.

Few firms or industries are immune from the effects of innovation, but it may have a very different character in different cases. From the strategic point of view the most significant characteristic is probably the frequency with which it occurs. In some industries innovation may come in large, discrete steps while in others it may appear as a continuous series of gradual accretions. A firm may try to target either or both of these approaches, but the appropriate choice will depend on the context. It may also be condi-

tioned by the firm's size, and in turn innovation may impact on th
relationships between large and small firms.

These issues are considered in Chapter 6.

Mergers

Firms grow and decline and may enter or exit different industries. But
decline or exit need not lead to closure if the units can be sold, and growth
or entry need not require new building if capacity can be acquired from
other firms. The choices between internal growth and acquisition, and
between mergers and looser forms of alliance are clearly strategic decisions,
and may be tied up with other aspects of strategy such as diversification or
innovation. But it is also apparent that mergers are more common in
Europe or America than they are in Japan, for example, and in general
alliances between firms are sometimes seen as an alternative to merger,
although this trend is more prevalent in some industries than in others.

These issues are considered in Chapter 7.

Networks

While the issues given above will provide the main content for the following
chapters, there is a sixth issue which runs between them like a connecting
web: that is the question of networks, or relations between firms which go
beyond formal contracts and into bonds of trust and mutual assistance. The
networks provide an alternative framework for business activity which lies
between the open market and the closed organisation. They may vary from
joint ventures or alliances, through licensing agreements and franchises, to
loose informal arrangements for the exchange of information or other forms
of co-operation. They are perhaps most commonly concerned with international operations, marketing or purchasing, and technology transfer.

The importance of networking has generally been increasing, but networks have always been of particular significance for firms from Asia
Pacific. It has long been recognised that a group orientation is more
favoured and individualism is less favoured in Asian cultures than they
are in America or Northern Europe (Hofstede, 1980). This has significant
implications for the characteristics of firms. In Japan, for example, a firm's
characteristics will depend heavily on its relations with other firms. Many
Japanese firms are interconnected through a *keiretsu* system in which they
maintain longstanding links which may or may not be reinforced by cross-
shareholding. Within the *keiretsu*, each individual firm remains largely
independent, but there is a feeling of common purpose and common
strategies are encouraged by frequent meetings, exchanges of personnel
and even by the use of a common name, as in the case of Mitsubishi.
Lasserre and Schütte (1995) estimated that about 60 per cent of the

companies quoted on the Tokyo stock exchange are affiliated in some way with one or other of the six very large *keiretsu* – Mitsubishi, Mitsui, Sumitomo, Fuyo, Daiichi-Kangyo and Sanwa.

A different form of networking which may nevertheless have very similar effects occurs among the Overseas Chinese Conglomerates, a group of companies in South-east and East Asia run by entrepreneurs of Chinese origin who maintain very strong links within their community. The firms are characterised, *inter alia*, by autocratic centralised leadership and a network of family and personal contacts through which the entrepreneurs obtain and test information (Lasserre and Schütte, 1995, pp. 100–6).

Similar networks have been increasing in Europe and America but are still less intense than in Asia Pacific. They may also be of a very different character. It is often suggested that Western networks arise as a consequence of strategic decision whereas in Asia the strategic decisions arise as a consequence of the networks.

Summary

These tensions within strategic thinking may be summarised as follows:

• Flexibility	versus	Economies of Scale
• Outsourcing	versus	Vertical Integration
• Focus	versus	Diversification
• Continuous Innovation	versus	Managed Innovation
• Internal Growth	versus	Acquisition & Merger
• Networking	versus	Independence

A simplistic view of strategy might suggest a consistent liking for the left-hand side in each of these conflicts, but strategic wisdom must involve a search for balance. The factors which affect that balance will be discussed in Chapters 3–7 below, but before that the next chapter continues with a short review of the way in which strategic thinking has responded to past changes in the business environment.

2   Developments in Strategic Thinking

INTRODUCTION

Business strategy is as old as business, but it is only quite recently that strategic thinking has been identified as a separable field of study. The first explicit references in the literature appear to date from the late 1950s (for example, Ewing, 1958), and early development owed much to works like Christensen *et al.* (1965) which sought to present a holistic view to replace the earlier dependence on separate functional specialisms. Since then, the norms of strategic behaviour have changed dramatically, primarily as a response to changes in the business environment but also as a consequence of progressive learning by strategic analysts.

It might be argued that strategic thinking is concerned with looking forward to an uncertain future and should therefore spare no time for looking back at the different circumstances which existed in the past. On the other hand it may be possible to gain valuable insights from past mistakes – those of us who do not understand the past may suffer when we try to repeat it. It may also be easier to understand recent trends such as the decline of conglomerates if we can first understand the different conditions which led to their growth. And it is always important to understand that the different models of strategic behaviour were designed in response to particular trends and problems and should never be used without a full understanding of their context. This does not necessarily mean that they are wrong: they may have been correct at the time and may still be useful in appropriate conditions. It does mean that they have to be used with care.

For the purposes of this review, the years since the 1950s may be divided very roughly into two periods, each of which has two sub-periods. The first period saw a common focus on the benefits of mass production and a concern to build a portfolio of business activities. It may be divided quite loosely into two sub-periods by an increasing concern for quality: both quality of output and quality or balance within the strategic portfolio. During the second period, the earlier emphasis on scale and unit costs gave way to a search for more diverse sources of competitive advantage and an increasing concern with the core business of the firm. Over time, however, the initial emphasis on leanness and flexibility has been complemented by a growing interest in potential developments into future markets, and this has reopened interest in the scope of the firm's activities.

It is tempting to equate these periods and sub-periods with precise intervals of calendar time, using a decade or thereabouts for each sub-period and a watershed around 1980 to separate the two periods. But life is never so precise. Some firms would still be focused on one phase long after others had moved on to the next; discussions in the literature sometimes preceded but often lagged behind the best business practice; and developments in America, Asia and Europe sometimes proceeded by different routes at different rates. It is probably wiser simply to recognise that there are overlapping phases of uncertain length, and then to concentrate on the nature of the changes regardless of their timing.

PHASE 1: THE DOMINANCE OF TECHNOLOGY

During the 1950s and into the 1960s, business was conditioned first by shortages caused by the Second World War, and then by a clamour for goods and services as people came to believe in an inexorable rise in their standards of living. In the times of extreme shortage almost any product was satisfactory so long as it was available, and as living standards began to rise standardised goods for the masses replaced bespoke products for the rich in many trades. Management was often little more than an exercise in logistics: how to amass resources to deliver a product as cheaply as possible. Capital markets were imperfect and tightly regulated so that retained profits and/or longstanding contacts with financial institutions were often the only feasible sources of capital, and this tilted the balance of competition in favour of established firms.

Large Size

These business conditions favoured those who already had access to the limited resources which were available, and encouraged them to find ways to get the best out of those resources. The main strategic tools for this were Economies of Scale and the Experience Curve. Each of these was taken to show how increases in output could lead to reductions in unit costs, or improvements in productivity, and for this reason they are sometimes confused. Logically, however, they are quite separate. One depends on the current rate of output and the other on the cumulative output produced. They are therefore as different as the speed of a car at any moment is different from the total distance travelled during a journey.

Economies of Scale

Economies of scale are defined as the extent to which the rate of output may be increased with a less than proportionate increase in resources, after allowing for appropriate adjustments to capacity. They will lead to reductions in unit costs so long as the gains in productivity are not offset by increases in the prices of resources. The gains are determined primarily by numerical or technological relationships. For example, random occurrences become more predictable in large samples; supertankers are more cost-effective because of numerical relationships between the capacity and the surface area of vessels; and some activities involve indivisible investments or set-up costs which can be apportioned between more and more units as output is increased.

Technologists may exploit these numerical relationships, but managers cannot alter them. If economies of scale are believed to be important, management's primary function is to provide the conditions for their exploitation. Large engineering plants will not be efficient if they are made to stand idle at frequent intervals while settings are changed to meet different product specifications. Their use must therefore be managed to ensure standardisation. Similarly supertankers can only be used efficiently if there is a need to carry large volumes over particular routes. Management must therefore ensure that the appropriate volumes are generated by their business and that appropriate facilities for loading, unloading and onward distribution are in place to exploit the potential cost advantages.

The logic of these arguments led to particular strategies. Large absolute size and high concentration in particular markets became clear strategic objectives, and were coupled with organisational design which emphasised the increasing specialisation of functions and the structure of work into simple, repetitive tasks which could be planned and tightly controlled. An apparently insatiable demand for standardised goods meant that the potential inflexibility of large unwieldy systems did not appear to be an issue at the time.

Experience

This approach to strategy was reinforced by arguments based on the experience curve, which predicted that the unit cost of output would fall as the cumulative output increased. The first formal recognition of experience or learning effects in production came from the aircraft industry in the 1920s when it was observed that, regardless of the rate of production, unit costs fell by approximately 20 per cent with every doubling of the cumulative output produced, as employees became more and more familiar with the tasks involved in the assembly of a complex product. Subsequently the reductions in cost achieved through learning-by-doing were observed for many manufacturing processes and seen to extend to non-manufacturing activities: just as skilled workers become more adept with experience, so managers learn to respond more quickly and accurately as the context becomes more familiar (see, for example, Abernethy and Wayne, 1974). This observed relationship between unit costs and cumulative output was then generalised into a strategic objective of increasing market share in order to gain more rapidly from learning-by-doing and thus steal a permanent advantage over competitors.

Managerial Preferences

These strategic arguments for growth and concentration may have been reinforced by managers' own preferences. It is frequently argued that salaried managers will seek to pursue their own objectives unless they are constrained by market competition and/or effective control by shareholders. In the absence of such constraints they may well pursue their own aims of power and influence, perks and prestige which might depend more on the size of their firm than on its immediate profitability. Theoretical explorations of such behaviour found their expression in the sales revenue maximising model (Baumol, 1959) and the managerial preference model, which allows explicitly for empire building through (say) excessive staff recruitment (Williamson, 1964).

Growth and Diversification

The incentives and the strategic guidelines coincided to produce a search for growth, which led on to a search for diversification. For example, in the United Kingdom between the early 1950s and the late 1960s, among the largest companies as measured by their sales in 1969–70, the proportion who depended on a single product line for 70 per cent or more of their sales fell from two-thirds to one-third (Channon, 1973). Similar long-term trends were observed in America, France, Germany and Italy (Dyas and Thanheiser, 1976; Rumelt, 1974; Scott, 1973).

Conglomerate mergers during this period were apparently encouraged by wide variations in management skills which were not corrected by other competitive pressures, and offered quick gains to corporate raiders who could see the potential value of the under-utilised assets. More general strategic arguments for diversification were sometimes presented in terms of the Product Life Cycle and Gap Analysis.

The Product Life Cycle

The Product Life Cycle was based on generalised observation and was assumed to describe the life cycle of a product or industry in terms of five stages: (i) the launch stage, when the product is first introduced to the market, often with intense promotion, but sales only grow slowly as potential customers come to learn about the product and make their first sample purchases; (ii) the early growth stage of rapid expansion as new customers are attracted to the product in significant numbers; (iii) the later growth stage of slower, less frenetic, growth; (iv) the maturity stage, when sales level off to cover repeat purchases and any gains from new customers are offset by the loss of older customers; and (v) the decline stage, during which more and more customers are enticed away to alternative products. In this form the details are too imprecise to be useful: the general shape of the cycle tells us nothing about the achievable sales volumes nor their timing; and the general shape may be misleading if the maturity stage can be postponed by a successful relaunch of the product or if an unsuccessful product collapses during its launch stage. Nevertheless the model was often taken as indicating that it may be dangerous to target sustained growth on the strength of a narrow product range, and also to suggest that sustained growth could only be based on a number of products or industries at different stages of their life cycles.

Gap Analysis

Given that the Product Life Cycle suggests a need for periodic diversification, Gap Analysis might then be used to determine its extent and timing. At its simplest, the analysis merely suggests that a firm should diversify when it cannot achieve its goals with its existing product range. This was then developed into a series of steps:

(1) set overall performance goals
(2) forecast outcomes for existing activities with current policies
(3) determine gap between goals and forecast
(4) review and revise policies for existing activities
(5) determine gap between goals and revised forecasts
(6) specify profile of new activities required to fill any gap
(7) consider resources available to generate revised profile
(8) determine diversification strategy.

Note that this sequence is problem-driven. It assumes that managers are reactive and that diversification is only undertaken to fill the gap when all else fails. There is no suggestion that new opportunities might be considered alongside existing activities before the gap emerges, although in practice a progressive firm might be expected to identify new opportunities through research or market contacts before it was pushed into doing so by a poor forecast. Nevertheless such a firm might still use Gap Analysis as a guide to the timing of diversification and to the sales volume which it had to set as a target for the new line of business.

Such a combination of limited prospects in older areas and research-based opportunities in new areas would certainly be consistent with American data for the period, provided we accept that further growth would become more difficult as an industry becomes more highly concentrated. Gort (1962) looked at the level of diversification among firms in American manufacturing industry in 1954. He found positive and statistically significant relationships between diversification and earlier measures of both concentration and technical activity, suggesting that firms with high levels of technical activity in concentrated industries were more likely to diversify as research generated new ideas to be exploited in other industries and as firms sought to grow without aggravating competition with their entrenched rivals.

United Kingdom data generally confirm the significance of research for diversification (Gorecki, 1975) but fail to disclose any statistically significant relationship between diversification and concentration. This is at variance with Gort's American study. The differences might possibly suggest that concentration is less appropriate as an indicator of limited growth opportunities in a market such as the United Kingdom with a greater dependence on international trade, or that by the later period covered by Gorecki (1963 rather than 1953) firms had come to anticipate potential restrictions on specialised growth and were building research-based diversification into their strategic planning from the outset.

'Blue Skies'

The trend towards diversification continued for some time (for a UK summary, see Clarke, 1985), but it is probably true that in the first sub-period of our history the areas chosen for diversification were as likely to be chosen for their intrinsic attractiveness as for any comparative advantage which the firm might be able to offer to the new area, and there were disparaging references to 'blue skies' diversification which suggested that firms acted as if they sought a sunny spot without reference to the cost of getting there nor to the overcrowded conditions which they might find when they arrived (Levitt, 1962).

At the time, however, the competitive constraints seemed to be insignificant. The established firms had favourable access to resources and could believe that their profits depended on where they chose to apply those resources rather than on any other comparative advantage which they might have. In this they were generally supported by statistical analysis which tended to associate profitability with the structure of different industries (concentration, barriers to entry, and so on) rather than the characteristics of different firms. It was not until later that attention came to be focused on intra-industry variations in profitability (see below, pages 33–4). Further, the increasing professionalism of managers may also have encouraged them to believe that they could cope with diversity, because professional management was then seen as a general skill which was applicable to any industry. The apparent conflict between this belief and the simultaneous emphasis on learning-by-doing was more apparent than real: managers generally believed that their learning in one industry could be transferred to other industries without loss, and that acquired skills in technology or marketing would help to overcome any barriers to entry and ensure long-term dominance in their target industries.

The transferability of skills between industries will be considered further in Chapter 5 below, but we may note immediately that 'blue skies' behaviour is not dead. For example it reappeared in the early 1990s in the market for memory chips, the tiny pieces of computer hardware which are used in products as diverse as personal computers and photocopiers. A significant shortage of production capacity at the time left demand unsatisfied and forced up prices. Profit margins rose and were reported to be in the region of 80 per cent. Thefts of memory chips became a significant threat in many industrial and commercial organisations. There was then a scramble to increase capacity, and in spite of the high absolute costs of new plant, several new suppliers entered by diversification. These included, for example, Taiwanese food and plastics companies. By 1996 the excess demand had disappeared, prices had fallen by up to 70 per cent, and it was reported that some of the new plants had to be mothballed (*The Economist*, 9 November 1996).

PHASE 2: THE SEARCH FOR QUALITY

The second phase continued the emphasis on economies of scale, standardisation and technocratic diversification, but qualified it with an increasing concern for quality. This focused on the quality of output, but was paralleled by increasing attention to the notion of quality or balance within a firm's strategic portfolio, and a growing awareness of the variety of pressures which could coexist in a competitive environment.

Quality of Output

During the first phase quality was often sacrificed on the altar of productivity as firms sought to increase output without paying enough attention to the possible consequences for the quality of that output. Towards the end of that phase, however (say, by about the end of the 1960s), the markets' reaction against shoddy and unreliable goods had become tangible, and firms were forced to show an increasing concern for the quality of their products. Gradually they came to accept that quality depended on individual, local initiatives which might well be stifled by centralised planning, and quality control procedures based upon negative sanctions were progressively replaced by quality assurance procedures based upon positive incentives. These changes began to call into question the ruling systems of hierarchical control and laid the foundation for later moves towards re-engineering and delayering (see Chapter 3).

At the same time there was an extensive debate about what a 'market oriented' firm should look like, and this started to erode the earlier emphasis on functional specialisation by encouraging closer co-operation between the marketing and manufacturing functions within firms.

A Balanced Portfolio

Questions of portfolio balance were addressed by the growth/share matrix promoted by the Boston Consulting Group and commonly known as the BCG Matrix. This categorises all products or business areas by reference to two characteristics: the growth rate of the market and the firm's relative share of that market. A common form of the matrix is illustrated in Figure 2.1.

The basic assumption is that mavericks must either be converted into stars or they must be abandoned, while dogs should be abandoned as soon as they become a drain on resources. Stars and those mavericks which are supported may be profitable, but they will consume resources for investment if they are to achieve their full potential and they must therefore be supported by the dull but worthy cows.

Various refinements to the model were developed in order to extend the definition of market attractiveness and to improve on market share as the sole measure of the firm's competitive position. For example, the competitive position might be defined as strong or weak after considering some combination of relative size, market share, relative product quality and relative production efficiency, while the definition of an attractive market might be extended beyond market growth to include market size, the availability of substitutes and the bargaining power of buyers or suppliers.

The concepts of the model were simple but the BCG Matrix was probably the best known strategic tool of the 1970s and it underpinned much strategic thinking. It probably encouraged diversification through its emphasis on the use of cash cows to fund stars or mavericks, which might be loosely equated with new ventures. Sadly, the model says little about the type of new venture which might be appropriate and it includes no reference to the competencies which would be needed for success. It may also blind firms to the need for

Firm's competitive position

		High share	Low share
Market attractiveness	High growth	STAR	MAVERICK
	Low growth	CASH COW	DOG

Figure 2.1 *Growth/share matrix*

action to protect the cash flow from their cows, which may quickly be displaced by competition if they are simply exploited without any thought for the future. Finally, it seems too ready to damn the dogs. In practice, the areas which are growing more slowly may need improved management rather than less management, especially if they are a significant part of the corporate business and are not readily saleable. As we shall see , the case for divestment comes more from a lack of congruence and excessive resource demands rather than simply from slow growth. Hammeresh and Silk (1979) in particular, stressed that firms may do well in stagnant or slow-growing markets if they accept the reality of slow growth and increased competition but also recognise that there may still be many unexplored opportunities. Continued growth may be possible if growth segments can be found within declining markets (as cinemas grew in American shopping centres even as the total number of cinemas declined); or if improved quality can attract a premium price from the remaining customers; or if cost effectiveness allows increased penetration into a static market (as in the manufacture of private label brands for retailers of slow-moving consumer goods). For these reasons the basic matrix was never more than a starting point for further discussion. Further, in a modern context the emphasis on cash cows may seem to be excessive because improved capital markets have made firms relatively less dependent on internal funds for expansion. Nevertheless the matrix did raise questions which were very pertinent at the time, and firms generally benefited from the increased emphasis on portfolio analysis which focused attention on the quality or balance within the portfolio and not just on its size (see, for example, Haspeslagh, 1982).

Competitive Forces

The growing awareness that quality must be a component of mass-produced goods, and the associated concern with marketing products rather than selling them, were accompanied by a greater readiness to accept that strategy could not be developed in a competitive vacuum. This was implicit in the PIMS data (see page 8 above), and found forceful expression in Porter's (1980) distillation of industrial economics into five forces of competition. A simplified summary of the five forces is given in Figure 2.2, which portrays the simultaneous pressures as rivalry among existing producers, potential competition from future entrants to the industry or from producers of substitute products in different industries, and the bargaining strength of powerful buyers or suppliers. The simple format can be a powerful reminder of the dangers of focusing on only one of the dimensions of competition.

This readiness to adopt some features of industrial economics into strategic thinking also presaged a shift of attention away from a corporate strategy and towards a business-level strategy. The former emphasises a

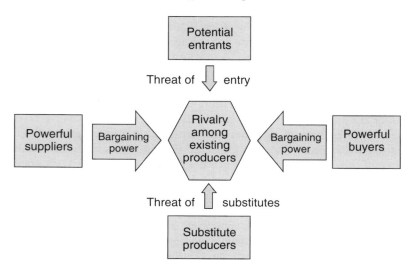

Figure 2.2   *Competitive forces*

holistic view of the corporation, while the business-level strategy focuses on distinct business areas and seeks to establish a sustainable competitive advantage in each area. In practice, the two approaches overlap, but it was the business level which was to dominate strategic thinking during the third phase of development.

PHASE 3: LEANNESS AND COMPETITION

The third phase saw the start of a movement away from large, diverse organisations towards lean structures built for rapid response. The driving force behind this change was a progressive but substantial increase in the nature and intensity of competition.

Global Changes in Competition

The changes may be summarised as follows:

- Trade barriers fell, moving competitive threats and reactions from a local to a global theatre.
- Capital became more mobile and better informed, reducing firms' dependence on local sources and increasingly forcing firms in different countries to compete for finance on the same terms.

- Many industries moved from a condition of excess demand to one of actual or potential excess capacity. At first this seemed to be largely a local problem, as, for example, European shipbuilders and steel producers faced new competition from Asia Pacific, but it has since become a global phenomenon in many industries.
- Local protection for firms or industries became less prevalent. Some national champions are still protected, most noticeably in the air transport or defence industries (see Chapter 7 below), but generally national governments are now more concerned to reduce than to increase the level of state subsidies, and have turned to the privatisation of publicly owned firms in order to improve their cash flow and encourage competition.
- Increasing affluence encouraged consumers to search for more variety. Global markets are not necessarily standardised markets and consumers generally sought more freedom to define the products and services they wanted. They were less inclined to accept the lowest common denominator offered by mass production, and the demand for products or services often came to include a demand for choice *per se*.

Lean Production

A demand for variety must be matched by operational and organisational flexibility if firms are to provide the choice of a full product range without sacrificing the efficiency and quality which are still essential for competitive success (see, for example, Bolwijn and Kumpe, 1990). The system of 'lean' production which is most commonly used to meet these ends is often associated with the name of Toyota, the Japanese motor car manufacturer, and owes its origin to the time before Toyota became a global supplier when it was faced by limited but rapidly growing demand for differentiated products in its home market (for a convenient summary, see Cusumano, 1994). The system of lean production involves:

- 'just in time' production in small lots which are designed to match demand and not to anticipate it;
- component supplies which are synchronised with production in order to minimise inventory;
- simple systems for ordering and delivering parts; and hence
- geographical concentration for ease of communication between producer and supplier;
- multiskilled process workers who are able to respond to changes in production with the minimum of hierarchical supervision; and
- continuous incremental improvements facilitated by the small lot sizes.

Such a system of lean production is in marked contrast to the system of pre-planned, standardised production which ruled during Phase 1, and the transition from technical domination to demand domination generally made it more difficult for firms to take full advantage of any potential economies of scale. A simple example may help to reinforce this point. Consider a race between a horse and a man. The horse has all the advantages of size including speed and stamina, and in a flat race, although the man may react more quickly and get off to a flying start, he will soon be overtaken by the horse. The relative positions may be reversed, however, if the race is switched to the 110 metres hurdles, because here the intervals between the hurdles are adjusted to match the man's stride pattern rather than the horse's. The horse will never get into its stride, and the wise money will be on the man every time.

The contrasts between Phase 1 and Phase 3, however, are not just between long production runs of standardised products and short runs of variable products. The changes affected most aspects of organisation and control. In particular, the system of lean production requires the firm to make rapid responses to orders from customers and to obtain equally rapid responses from its suppliers. This is simply not possible with long feedback loops through central selling or purchasing agencies. Authority must be devolved to skilled workers who can take local initiatives, not only to ensure that orders from customers are met but also to introduce improvements in products or services or production techniques as soon as the need is recognised. These requirements reinforce the change from control to assurance which began in Phase 2, and have progressively undermined the old hierarchical systems of centralised control.

Note that the simplest systems of lean production may need to be modified for international firms with dispersed manufacturing facilities: geographical concentration of production and suppliers may be harder to achieve; suppliers in other countries may be less responsive; and less-skilled workers may need more supervision. In general an unthinking pursuit of leanness may make untenable assumptions about co-operation, or the readiness of employees to accept devolved responsibility, or the ability of suppliers to guarantee the deliveries which are needed for 'just in time' production, in the same way as the technocrats who advocate economies of scale and experience may make unrealistic assumptions about the motivation of customers and employees. Nevertheless the basic principles are still valid. They have been adopted widely throughout manufacturing industry, and the same principles of devolution to achieve rapid response and flexibility are increasingly common in service industries.

Firms' Conduct versus Industrial Structure

At the same time as firms have responded to changes in demand there has been a growing acceptance that the performance of firms is not governed simply by the characteristics of their industry but also by their own competencies and experience, which will change relatively slowly. This has been driven primarily by the changes in competition but it has also received clear support from theoretical and statistical analysis. It may be seen, for example, in economic analysis with the decline of 'structure' as the main focus of industrial economics. Under the structure/conduct/performance paradigm which ruled during the 1960s and into the 1970s, most industrial economists focused on anticipated relationships between performance (such as profits, costs, innovation) and structural variables such as concentration, entry and product differentiation. It was commonly assumed that the structure would change slowly and that the effects could be observed without separate reference to the motives or conduct of individual firms. From about the mid-1970s, however, industrial economists became increasingly dissatisfied with this approach, and began to investigate alternative models in which preferences, behaviour and technology combined to determine aspects of structure, and especially the concentration of sellers, jointly with prices, outputs and profits (see, for example, Cable, 1994).

Similar conclusions are suggested by statistical analyses of profit rates. The American Federal Trade Commission's Line of Business Programme is the only source of disaggregated data which separates the profits of diversified corporations into their component industries. The FTC collected the data for four years, 1974–7, with between 432 and 471 corporations reporting in any one year. Corporate data were disaggregated to business units and assigned to one of 261 (4-digit) categories of manufacturing industry. The average corporation reported on about 8 business units. Schmalensee used this data to analyse the larger business units in 1975 and concluded that a business unit's performance was dominated by the industry in which it operated (Schmalensee, 1985). This would be consistent with the view taken in Phases 1 and 2 above, which still dominated some thinking into the 1990s (see, for example, the introduction to Montgomery and Porter, 1991).

This view was rejected, however, by a more comprehensive study undertaken by Rumelt (1991), which included all four years of the FTC data to distinguish between stable and year-to-year components of the variance in profits. This suggested that 1975 had been an abnormal year in the series. The more stable effect indicated that business units differ from one another within industries much more than industries differ from one another. Furthermore, the dispersion of profit rates within industries was not explained significantly by market share nor by the corporate control of different business units in different industries. The data could not identify further possible explanations for the dispersion, but Rumelt suggested that his results were consistent with views of business strategy in which 'product-specific reputation, team-specific learning, a variety of first-mover advantages, causal ambiguity that limits effective imitation, and other special conditions permit equilibria in which competitors can earn dramatically different rates of return' (Rumelt, 1991, p. 180).

The FTC data are unique, but similar conclusions followed from studies which used corporate-level data. For example, Hansen and Wernerfelt (1989), using a sample of 60 of the 1,000 largest American firms, suggested that a firm's portfolio of activities was less important for its profitability than were its unique characteristics as indicated by its 'concern for welfare' and 'goal commitment'. Alternatively, using a different methodology but implying similar conclusions, Cubbin and Geroski's (1987) investigation of a dynamic model of the profitability of firms in the United Kingdom over the period 1951–77, indicated that nearly half the firms in the sample did not share in their industry's 'common' responses to dynamic changes.

The balance of evidence, therefore, is that it is firms and not industries which account for most differences in profitability, and this suggests that the 'blue skies' search for profitable industries must give way to a greater concern for distinctiveness in the strategic thinking of firms.

Niche Markets and Mobility Barriers

Coupled with this concern for distinctiveness came a reconsideration of the older, broader definitions of industry. Markets were divided into segments and distinctiveness was often equated with niche markets in which a firm could identify itself with the needs of a precisely defined sub-group of buyers. Similarly the long-established focus on entry barriers which may protect established firms from potential entrants was complemented by the notion of 'mobility barriers' (Caves and Porter, 1977). These have the same origins in cost advantages or product differentiation, but focus on the features within a market which may prevent established firms from pursuing particular paths and/or may protect firms which occupy particularly favoured positions, just as fissures may separate walkers on the apparently smooth surface of a glacier. They suggest that the conditions which deter new entrants may also affect the growth of established firms. For example, the relationship between Manx Airlines and British Airways (page 60 below) suggests that mobility barriers may protect both the regional carriers and the international airlines from penetration into each other's markets.

Mobility barriers may affect strategic thinking in either or both of two ways: the barriers may affect the pattern of growth or they may help to define competing groups.

Patterns of Growth

First, mobility barriers will influence the survival and growth of firms. Firms or business units which are established in a niche market may still not have ready access to other sub-markets within the same industry. If they are to grow they will first need to establish a larger bridgehead, which depends on the gradual accumulation of goodwill and production expertise. As a firm crosses the threshold into further niches it may be relatively exposed to competition until it becomes established, but if it is successful it will then find that the mobility barriers become less hazardous for further expansion into other sub-markets. (For an extended discussion, see Geroski, 1991.)

Competing Groups

Secondly, mobility barriers may serve to define competing groups. As a firm seeks to position itself within an industry it accumulates a distinct set of assets such as brand names, distribution channels, capital equipment, research capability, competencies and networks of relationships. Other firms which have followed similar strategies will have accumulated similar assets. These assets take time to acquire and may therefore act as mobility barriers protecting the group against imitation, but they may also lock the members of the group into certain types of strategic behaviour, and ensure that any new opportunities may be exploited only by the firms from a particular strategic group whose assets most closely resemble those needed for the new area. An industry may then comprise more than one such strategic group, and each group may be expected to react differently to changes in market conditions. For example, McGee and Segal-Horn (1990) identified four strategic groups in the European food processing industry: Multinational Major Branders such as Unilever or Heinz; National Major Branders who may be local brand leaders for a fairly narrow product range; Minor National Branders who do not aspire to brand leadership but may venture into other national markets; and National Own Label Suppliers.

A proper awareness of entry and mobility barriers ought to inform any firm's strategic decisions, and should reinforce the rejection of 'blue skies' policies which consider only the superficial attractiveness of different areas.

PHASE 4: RESPONSIVENESS AND INNOVATION

Continuous Innovation

The fourth and, for the moment, the final phase sees further responses to the market demands for variety and leanness. Consumers' search for uniqueness in the midst of variety is reflected back to suppliers of products and services as a continuous demand for innovation. As we shall see in Chapter 4, this reinforces the need for close working relationships with suppliers. It also changes the focus of much innovation away from central and separate research departments towards *ad hoc*, multidisciplinary teams with fluid lines of command (see Chapter 6). But as innovation becomes less structured it also becomes more difficult to control. A firm must create a cultural environment which accepts learning and change, but it must also ensure that the organisation is protected from the possible side-effects of uncontrolled innovation. Managers must learn to balance entrepreneurship and control.

A Lean Portfolio

Starting during the third phase and increasingly during the fourth phase the principle of leanness was extended from production into the firm's portfolio of activities. Conglomerate structures became more difficult to justify once it was accepted that success might depend upon resources and competencies which were specific to each business area, and that a central office might add little but an administrative burden to the operations of separable business units. The emphasis on separate businesses might then be reinforced by increasing local accountability under which activities which were once 'staff' functions in head office were transferred further towards the sharp end of business operations.

These trends were not universal, but in many cases there was an increased emphasis on 'focus' as a source of competitive advantage. Successful firms were expected to focus sharply on a limited number of core areas where they might have a defensible advantage, and to withdraw from other activities which might be at best a distraction and at worst a cancer which could destroy the organisation.

Note, however, that the term 'core' may be subject to two different and potentially contradictory interpretations. As 'core business' it may imply a narrow focus on a limited range of products, services or markets. This may be beneficial if it encourages the firm to concentrate resources which might otherwise be dispersed over too many different activities. But it may also prove to be a restriction if it means that the firm ignores opportunities or threats in other areas which may eventually undermine its core. It may then prove to be the equivalent of a military strategy which always knows how to win the last war but is still digging in for trench warfare while the blitzkrieg rolls over the top. On the other hand, if the core is defined in terms of core competencies rather than core products, it will emphasise the particular skills or combinations of resources which are the specific attributes that distinguish one firm from another. This gives a wider perspective, and a proper analysis of core competencies may sometimes lead towards new opportunities which might otherwise seem to be unrelated to the existing core products.

Business statements on strategy in the 1990s commonly emphasise a concentration on core activities and the contracting out of non-core and non-competent activities. In some cases the restructuring which this implies may only buy time for more creative strategic thinking, but the focus on core activities has led to widespread downsizing, re-engineering, divestment and outsourcing as major facets of strategic positioning, in marked contrast to the earlier emphasis on size and diversification. The significance of resource endowments and competencies for the focus of a firm will be discussed in Chapter 5 below (see especially pages 92–7).

OVERVIEW: THREE ELEMENTS

Strategic thinking is now undoubtedly more complex than it appeared to be in the 1950s and 1960s, and is usually compounded of some mix of three elements: focus, flexibility and future development.

Focus

The emphasis on focus reflects the imperative for a firm to concentrate on the things it does best. This is clearly true for the range of activities undertaken by the corporation as a whole, but it is no less true of the competitive strategy pursued by each business unit. Porter, for example, has argued that strategy is about finding the position in the market which best exploits the firm's capabilities (Porter, 1980). He offered three generic strategies which might lead to a competitive advantage, and warned that a confused mix of these strategies could lead to disaster. From this perspective a firm might target cost leadership if it has the breadth to achieve some economies of scale coupled with comparative advantages in technology or material supplies; it might seek differentiation and offer unique attributes to buyers, provided that uniqueness is not bought at too high a cost; and in either case the strategy may be applied with a broad focus or within narrow market segments. The approach has been criticised as simplistic (for example, Bowman, 1992) but it does effectively emphasise the dangers of being out of focus, and so losing mass markets to lower-cost producers while simultaneously failing to offer unique products for recognisable market niches.

Flexibility

Flexibility became paramount during the third and fourth phases of development. If it is pursued immoderately it may create instability and become 'management by destruction', but an attempt to create a responsive organisation is now an essential feature of strategic thinking at all levels of business. For example, Peters (1987) argued that firms should target market creation and not market share, and should create high-value-added products for niches which are desired and understood by customers in a process of continuous transformation. Successful organisations are seen as lean organisations and need skilled, flexible staff who are responsive to change and innovation, committed to quality and service, and ready to work in autonomous units in non-hierarchical structures.

Future

The final element of strategy must be a concern for future development. This suggests that if strategy is concerned solely with competitive positioning in existing markets it will be condemned to a reactive and not a proactive role. Leading firms are those which have taken charge of the transformation of their industry by challenging the rules of engagement, redrawing market boundaries or creating new industries (Hamel and Prahalad, 1994). Future leadership requires current action to understand the trends and discontinuities which will create new strategic space; to develop competencies; to attract coalition partners; to create infrastructures; and to prove alternative products and service concepts which will provoke favourable responses from consumers.

These three elements – competitive focus, flexibility and future development – must be combined in any successful strategy. They are the implicit underpinnings for the discussion in the following chapters.

3 Size and Rationalisation

INTRODUCTION

Chapter 2 showed how the emphasis on technocratic management and economies of scale, which dominated strategic thinking during the 1950s and 1960s, has given way progressively to greater emphasis on quality, flexibility and innovation. Lean production and devolution now dominate manufacturing and the same principles have extended well into the service industries.

This chapter will look at the balance between flexibility and scale in more detail. It considers the problems and looks at some of the changes which may help to secure a reasonable balance. It also notes that a number of strategic reservations may be made against the headlong pursuit of flexibility.

This leads on to the different strengths and weaknesses of large, medium and small firms and the way in which their different resource bases should be reflected in different strategies. These differences point to the complementarity of firms of different size, which must be reflected further in their strategies.

ENDURING ADVANTAGES OF SIZE

Economies of Scale

The nature of economies of scale was discussed in general terms on pages 22–3 above. These advantages may arise in any or all of the firm's operations; in purchasing, distribution, marketing and research, for example, as well as in production. The technical economies in production are most likely to be realised when output is concentrated in a single plant which can exploit specialist facilities to their full potential. However, if the technical economies are not significant and the size of plant is limited by geographical factors such as the availability of inputs or the dispersion of markets, a firm may combine several plants in order to exploit economies of scale in (say) marketing or research.

Further, a firm may be able to exploit economies of scope by combining two or more different and separable products. This may arise simply because the products are related in some way, as the combination of different food products or different articles of clothing which have different seasonal peaks in demand may provide a more regular flow of work throughout the year for a firm's sales and distribution facilities. From the point of view of its influence on the size of firms, however, the main relevance of economies of scope is that the combined outputs of two or more products may enable a firm to exploit potential economies of scale in activities like administration, distribution or research which are at least partly directed at aggregate sales and not just at the sales of individual products. In principle, this might be achieved by increasing the diversity within a single plant, but Gollop and Monahan (1991) suggested that economies of scope are more effective when central activities support a series of plants which individually retain the benefits of specialisation.

In any particular case, the potential economies of scale will be determined by the technical characteristics of the means of production. However, as we saw in Chapter 2, a firm's ability to exploit any potential economies will depend upon the level or pattern of demand which it faces, and in recent years the general pattern has changed from one of standardisation and cost reduction to one of variety and value added (see page 31 above). This has not eliminated economies of scale, but it has meant that the potential applications have to be looked at more carefully than seemed to be necessary in the past.

As a first step we might say that the increased demand for variety and flexibility has often reduced firms' freedom to exploit technical economies of scale in production, because it has become more difficult to use specialised, indivisible facilities which need long production runs to achieve their full potential. On the other hand, the changes are less likely to have undermined any size-related economies of scope. The nature of the corporate-wide activities which give rise to such economies may have altered (see, for example, Chapter 6 below), but the potential advantages of scale in (say) marketing or research, remain. Indeed, if anything their impact on performance may have become relatively more important as the significance of purely technical economies has declined.

Further, although the design of finished products may have become less standardised, this does not necessarily apply to all the components which go into those products. Considerable variety may be achieved with standardised components, and in general the scope for standardisation will be much greater for basic materials and unassembled components than it is for sub-assemblies or finished products. The design of cylinder blocks in motor cars, heating elements in electric kettles, zips in jeans, for example, is not necessarily affected by variations in the design of the finished product. In some cases, the persistent exploitation of scale economies for standard components may even help to increase the choices available to consumers. In personal computers, for example, although large suppliers continue to dominate the market, the ready availability of standard components – motherboards, VDUs, disc drives and so on – coupled with the ubiquity of IBM-compatibility and Microsoft software, has enabled smaller assembly firms to draw components from a number of different manufacturers in order to supply particular local markets.

In general we should expect that economies of scale in production will continue to be significant whenever there is a large demand for standardised products which use standardised inputs. Typically these conditions predominate in the manufacture of basic synthetic materials and in the extraction and refining of bulk minerals. In the manufacture of bulk chemicals, for example, a 50 per cent increase in the capacity of a new ethylene cracker, from 400,000 to 600,000 tonnes per annum, might yield unit cost reductions of around 20 per cent. In cases like this, the scale of production is a primary source of strategic advantage and those firms which cannot achieve the requisite scales are forced out of the manufacture of basic materials into later stage processing and/or into niche markets. Several chemical firms have had to accept this alternative, recognising that they are relatively small players in a large global industry. For example, ICI, which is Britain's largest chemical group, has changed its focus to concentrate on speciality chemicals, and has sold off most of the business units which dealt with bulk products (see also page 136 below).

Stature

In other cases even though there may be few technical economies of scale in production, the trend towards globalisation may favour firms which are large enough to offer products or services on a global scale. We might refer to this as the firm's stature rather than its scale. The potential advantages include the ability to bring together a large pool of financial resources, possibly a powerful brand, worldwide networks and perhaps even political influence.

Consider, for example, the firms specialising in international reinsurance, which accept insurance business from the primary insurers who sell insurance to the general public, and so enable risks to be spread so that the impact of an exceptional loss or series of losses can be borne more easily. The case for increased stature has grown with globalisation and with increases in the losses caused by natural catastrophes, for which the insured losses will increase as the industry becomes more successful and more sophisticated even if the incidence of catastrophes does not change. The primary insurers look for greater financial strength from their reinsurers and also expect a degree of sophisticated expertise of the sort which is provided more readily in larger organisations which can cover a range of specialisms. In their turn the reinsurers will gain by covering a number of different types of risk in several different countries because, unlike the primary insurers, they cannot lay off the risks they carry. These considerations have encouraged larger size and led to increased concentration. In 1996, for example, the third largest American reinsurer, American Re, was acquired by the German firm, Munich Re, which was then already the world's largest reinsurer, while Swiss Re (formerly Schweizer Rück), which claimed to be the world's leading life and health reinsurer after its acquisition of Mercantile and General Re in 1996, went on to acquire Unione Italiana di Riassicurazione and Francaise de Réassurances to strengthen its position in Europe still further.

Similar considerations of stature led to mergers between large accountancy firms in the mid-1990s, and were also reflected in the combinations between advertising agencies in the 1980s, as the agencies sought global stature to match the perceived needs of some of the large advertisers, and to offer global consistency and a more rapid cross-fertilisation between different markets. These combinations often formed multi-agency groups under a form of holding organisation, including WPP, the world's largest, Omnicom, Interpublic and the UK-based Cordiant. The moves have been further encouraged by firms like IBM and Reckitt & Colman, the British supplier of soaps and polishes, who have looked for a single agency to handle all their advertising.

However, the arguments are not all in favour of large stature. For example, Procter & Gamble, the world's largest advertiser, prefers to divide its expenditure between more than one agency in order to preserve the stimulus of competition and take advantage of the diverse skills of different agencies, and a large agency may face potential conflicts of interest when it bids for the accounts of clients who produce competing products. Further, the group agencies may be burdened by the overheads imposed by the parent company, which are estimated to cost between 1 and 1.5 per cent of revenue. The successful groups believe that this is justified by increased efficiency in handling tax and other financial matters, and by adding value through collaboration in training, information technology and practice development. But the advantages cannot be guaranteed, they must be managed. Continued failure to form a coherent group forced Cordiant to demerge in 1997 into three independently managed businesses – Saatchi and Saatchi, Bates, and Zenith (a media services group).

PROBLEMS OF SIZE

The example of Cordiant serves to emphasise the essential point that size may not be neutral if it does not give specific advantages: large stature may prove to be a hindrance when economies of scale are slight or uncertain.

Technical and Market Factors

Ultimately the only significant disadvantages of size are behavioural and rest with management or labour relations rather than technology or the market. It is true that technical diseconomies may be found in individual pieces of manufacturing plant and equipment, if a size is reached at which any further expansion would put intolerable stress on the materials from which the plant is built and/or require high-performance materials whose costs more than offset any potential gains. But such a limit on the size of plant will not imply any diseconomy for the firm as a whole if the plants can be duplicated or new products produced in new plants without loss of effective control. It could only be a failure in management which allowed the technical diseconomies to undermine the firm as a whole.

Similar arguments may be applied if the market is limited and cannot absorb the potential output of large units. Costs may then rise as additional transportation or marketing effort is needed to sell additional output, but the increase would then reflect management's decision to produce more than the market can absorb and it is not a diseconomy of scale *per se*. Markets may prevent the exploitation of economies of scale but they do not cause diseconomies.

A small market may still be a problem for a large firm, however, if the firm's size leads to accusations of monopoly or predatory behaviour. A firm which is both absolutely and relatively large, either in relation to a single market or in relation to the economy as a whole, might expect to attract more attention from a government concerned to preserve competition or from pressure groups concerned to protect particular aspects of social justice or the environment. The impact of any possible reactions from such groups must be part of the contextual analysis in the firm's strategic appraisal and may indicate that certain lines of development are unwise or undesirable. For example, it is frequently reported that Microsoft has rejected some apparent opportunities for diversification in an attempt to avoid provocation to the American Federal Trade Commission. Such a constraint may affect the direction chosen for growth, but it will rarely appear as an absolute limit to the size of the firm. It will only be in exceptional circumstances that a large firm will be subdivided into smaller units by government fiat, as when AT&T was forced to hive off its regional and local telephone service from 'Ma Bell' to seven separate 'Baby Bells' in 1982–3 after it lost an antitrust suit brought by the American government. Such considerations will hardly enter into the strategic thinking of most firms.

Behavioural Factors

By contrast the behavioural factors are potentially more pervasive and more certain. The purpose of management is to plan and implement change, whether that is change to correct deviations from planned routes or change to move in new directions along new routes. In the extreme, there would be no role for management if nothing ever changed and it was known that this state would continue for ever. If it is to effect change, management must have information about what is happening, sufficient knowledge to appraise and select alternatives, and the means to implement its choices. In large organisations both the initial flow of information and the instructions for implementation may be distorted as they are gathered or disseminated more widely through many people and through many layers in the organisation; and at the same time managers with bounded rationality may find it more difficult to handle some of the problems which become more complex as the organisation grows larger. As the problems increase, managers may spend more of their time on trying to make the system work and less on the true function of management. Individuals or groups within the organisation may recognise that they occupy key positions as 'gate keepers' for the flow of information and instructions or for the allocation of resources, and they may seek to exploit the position for their own aggrandisement, helping to produce a bureaucracy which pursues its own ends regardless of the needs of the organisation.

In all cases, but especially if the communications have to cross national boundaries, differences in language or technical jargon may make it more likely that the messages will not be understood, and differences in culture may mean that some of those which are understood are resisted. Individuals may then react with indifference, or with a sense of alienation which may be reinforced by the narrow repetitive tasks which are often required for efficient mass production. The alienation may then encourage restrictive practices, both as a defence against unwanted changes and as a collective attempt by the employees to reassure themselves that their work is still important.

Whether or not these effects are necessarily debilitating in the absence of weak management, is debatable. What is certain is that the significance of communication and motivation increases as firms try to become more flexible, responsive and innovative. Individual firms may survive for some time with top-heavy, over-hierarchical structures provided that their market power allows enough slack for them to tolerate the inefficiencies, and provided that the strategy which led to their dominant position is still appropriate. Problems arise when the context changes to deny these conditions. The organisation then needs new information, new understanding and a responsiveness to new commands. But the information and the responsiveness may not be there when they are needed if the problems of communication and co-ordination have been allowed to become acute, and the new understanding may be suppressed by an arrogant reluctance to learn. Like the courtiers surrounding the French King Louis XVIII at the time of the revolution, many firms find that as the context changes they are able to forget nothing and to learn nothing.

Behavioural Examples

Precise diagnosis of any individual case is difficult, but business history offers many examples of large firms which made mistakes that might have looked like poor judgement but which were almost certainly caused or worsened by some combination of arrogance, misinformation and loss of control.

IBM Corporation

Consider, for example, the case of the IBM Corporation which dominated the market for general purpose computer systems through the 1960s and 1970s, supplying 65–70 per cent of the total value of computers installed in the non-Communist world at that time. By the mid-1980s IBM retained 70 per cent of the market for mainframe computers but had a smaller share of 15–35 per cent of the smaller markets for mini- and microcomputers. It made the mistake, however, of assuming that strategies which had once been successful would always prove to be so. It concentrated on the market for 'heavy iron' – the mainframe market – and assumed that smaller computers were for first-time buyers who would progress to mainframes as soon as they were able to do so. IBM was therefore quite unprepared for the transition to networked personal computers which occurred in the early 1990s, and it suffered heavily as a result. Since then it has retained its dominance of the mainframe market where it has some protection because the very large initial outlays make a commitment to IBM very difficult to reverse once it has been taken. It also benefits from sales of mainframe software which exceed the sales of specialist software firms. But it has never recovered its earlier dominant position in the computer market as a whole.

Further examples of large firms which lose ground through inflexibility will be considered in Chapter 6, but we may note here that IBM's experience has been mirrored by that of its largest rival, the Japanese Fujitsu, which includes the American subsidiary Amdahl and the British ICL, which it acquired in 1990. Like IBM, Fujitsu kept its faith in mainframes and was ill-prepared for the growing use of networked personal computers in Japan, although unlike IBM it has been cushioned by its more diversified base which includes activities such as telecommunications and microchips.

McDonald's

Even when the initial strategy remains sound a firm may lose some of its relative position if it loses control over the implementation of that strategy, as appeared to happen to the McDonald's fast-food chain in the mid-1990s. McDonald's was founded in 1955 with a strategy of growth based on franchising, with some 90 per cent of its American outlets run by franchisees who accepted the company's very exacting requirements for quality, service and cleanliness. By the mid-1990s it had some 21,000 outlets worldwide and the second most famous brand name after Coca-Cola. It had pursued a successful policy of overseas expansion, but increased competition for fast foods from Burger King (owned by the British Grand Metropolitan company), Wendy's, and Taco Bell (part of the restaurant division of PepsiCo until 1997) led to stagnant or declining sales in America. Part of McDonald's initial response was an intensive development of niche markets, seeking to enter every niche which might offer opportunities to its competitors. The niches included restaurants or snack bars in hospitals, shops, universities and petrol stations, and extended to children's meals for United Airlines. Eventually, however, the rapid expansion of outlets which resulted from the intensive development of niches conflicted with its original strategy based on franchising and quality. Both the franchisees and the quality suffered. McDonald's faced commercial pressure to compensate some franchisees who lost out to the niche developments; the revised cooking instructions which it sent to franchisees in 1996 were seen as an implicit acknowledgement that standards had declined; and a series of changes in management structure were explicitly designed to lead back to a more devolved system.

A Reservation

Examples like these stand as a constant reminder to large firms of the potential dangers of inflexible arrogance and of the need for vigilance to avoid short or medium-term goals which may undermine strategic objectives. However, before we turn to consider the restructuring which may reduce some of the behavioural diseconomies of large scale and of hierarchical structures, we should note that there can never be any guarantee of permanent success: large firms may always be at risk from competitors who are able to follow their lead and pursue similar strategies more effectively from a more favourable resource base, just as the best athletes may find that their records are eventually broken by others who follow their example. For example, Japan's Nippon Steel is the world's largest producer of steel and it built its dominance on a strategy of cost leadership based on technical expertise, cheap capital and low-cost labour, supported by a surging domestic economy. Eventually the high value of the yen encouraged Nippon Steel to move much of its production overseas, and it was challenged increasingly by South Korea's Pohang Iron & Steel Company, which had also grown from a rapidly expanding domestic base with the same initial advantages of cheap capital and low-cost labour.

RESTRUCTURING AND RE-ENGINEERING

Restructuring in Principle

We have seen that the potential disadvantages of large size are most likely to affect hierarchical, functionally based structures which are faced with rapid change. The demand for flexibility and its accompanying call for leanness are common to all types of organisation. Where restructuring is required to provide this flexibility it will generally have two components: it will involve a reduction in the number of levels in the hierarchy and the replacement of functional units by interdisciplinary project teams.

In hierarchical organisations the different layers act as filters to process and store information and to interpret and transmit commands. When the system breaks down, the senior management may look for other structures which either eliminate the need for these tasks or enable them to be performed in different ways. If the multiple layers distort or delay the flow of information then the number of layers must be reduced. Information may then be processed and transmitted in some other way by the use of information technology, and the need to transmit and interpret commands can be reduced by devolution and local accountability. Those middle managers who retain control over the allocation of some key resource must be persuaded to see themselves as facilitators and not as controllers.

But there is also a proactive as well as a reactive element in the transition. Information technology allows information to be made available to all those who need to use it, and the devolution ensures that day-to-day decisions on scheduling and the deployment of resources to meet customers' immediate demands are taken effectively by those who are fully aware of the context in which the decision is to be implemented, and who assume responsibility for both the decision and the quality of the outcome.

Further, the constraints which get in the way of a rapid response are not caused only by the steps in a hierarchy but also by the paper curtain which separates different functional specialisms such as finance, engineering, purchasing and personnel. A flexible organisation cannot wait while a problem is passed between functional units acting like mediaeval guilds to preserve their autonomy. Tasks can often be undertaken more quickly and more effectively if the different specialisms are brought together into cross-functional teams whose existence is only coincident with that task and whose allegiance must be to the achievement of that task within the team and not to the norms of some separate functional group.

The changes which are needed to bring this about are likely to require extensive education and training to generate confidence and competence in the new procedures, and may depend upon the introduction of revised pay scales to recognise the greater accountability and responsibility of what were previously lowly levels within the hierarchy. The restructurings are often referred to as de-layering in order to emphasise the removal of at least one layer within the hierarchy, but the best of them involve a complete re-engineering of the firm's activities, based on a fundamental reappraisal of all its processes and controls.

Restructuring in Practice

Examples

As one example, consider the case of Siemens Nixdorf Service which provides worldwide computer-related services including installing, servicing, maintaining and networking computer software and hardware (for full details, see Obolensky, 1994). It generated revenue of over $2 billion per annum in the early 1990s, having been formed in the late 1980s in a merger between Siemens DI of Munich and Nixdorf of Paderborn. Increased competition with greater emphasis on service in general and after-sales service in particular prompted a review which led to a re-engineering programme starting in 1991. Of particular concern to the service organisation was the low productivity of service engineers, but it was recognised that any improvement would need both operational and organisational changes. The principal changes were a restructuring of 30 regions into 5 areas with two fewer hierarchical levels, and a regrouping of the field engineers into teams with additional specialist support staff, some of whom were redeployed from the Head Office. Head Office staff numbers were cut by 50 per cent and procedures were revamped to provide more direct support to the field teams; information technology was used to improve information flows; new diagnostic processes were introduced; and measurement and incentive schemes were changed to give a clearer focus on customers' needs. As the changes were introduced region by region the results typically included a significant increase in the 'first time fix rate' and improved customer satisfaction. Operating costs fell as the engineers were able to double the number of customers served per day. Employee numbers were reduced by 20 per cent.

In general, the successful introduction of flatter, team-based structures with enhanced local autonomy can have a dramatic impact on flexibility. In the late 1980s Hewlett Packard reduced the lead time between the receipt of an order and finished production of electronic testing equipment from four weeks to five days, and the development time for a new computer printer from 4.5 years to 1.8 years. Honda reduced the development time for new cars from five years to three years and the US General Electric Company reduced the order/production interval for circuit breakers from three weeks to three days (*Fortune* magazine, 13 February 1989, quoted by West, 1992).

Note, however, that the stultifying effects of hierarchical control are found not only between management and operating units but also between the centre and the different divisions of a complex organisation. Restructuring that focuses only on one set of relationships is unlikely to achieve a full resolution. Consider Hoechst, which is the sixth largest industrial organisation in Germany and Europe's largest chemical company. In 1996 Hoechst announced that it would break up into six legally separate subsidiaries, although most would remain as wholly owned, unquoted companies. Earlier the company had been so centralised that an average divisional manager had control over no more than 30 per cent of the division's costs. Changes were introduced in 1994 to eliminate cross-subsidisation between divisions, and the restructuring announced in 1996 was planned to ensure that each subsidiary would have operational independence from the holding company.

Downsizing

Clearly, restructuring may lead to improvements in productive efficiency. It may also involve substantial retraining and increased pay for those whose jobs are enhanced by the new working arrangements. However, the increased flexibility which improves the firm's operations may imply less job security and has certainly led to job losses in many cases. In 1996 the annual survey of the American Management Association which covered nearly 1,500 large and medium-sized firms, revealed that nearly half had eliminated jobs in the year 1995–6 and that of these the majority involved restructuring or re-engineering. Some individual changes of this nature may have a large impact on their sector: it is estimated that British retail banking lost 80,000 jobs to restructuring between 1989 and 1995, and a study of the UK water supply industry revealed that in the six years after privatisation, 1989–95, the ten leading English and Welsh water companies cut the numbers actually dealing with water by nearly 22 per cent, with a loss of more than 10,000 jobs.

In general, however, the aggregate figures for 'downsizing' are not easy to interpret. The American Management Association's survey also revealed that more than two-thirds of the firms surveyed had created some new jobs during the year, and more than a quarter of those which had eliminated jobs were nevertheless reporting net increases in employment as increased demand in some areas offset the losses in others. Further, in some cases the jobs which are lost through restructuring in one firm may reappear elsewhere, especially if the restructuring involves an increase in outsourcing (see Chapter 4) or in focus-driven divestment (see Chapters 5 and 7).

DELAYERING – SOME RESERVATIONS

Incentives

Restructuring may improve productivity, but as we have seen it also involves the redefinition and reappraisal of jobs and extensive retraining which may offset any immediate cost savings. Shallower structures also change employees' expectations about the possibility of promotion, and therefore the reward systems may have to be rethought and linked to lateral mobility in order to ensure that incentives can be preserved. Further, the process of downsizing may also create feelings of insecurity, especially if the first round of job losses is not expected to be the last, and the consequent loss of morale may then offset the potential improvements in efficiency and reduce the local concern for quality standards. At the margin, morale and monitoring are at least partially substitutable. Well-motivated staff will need less monitoring, whereas a drop in morale may require more monitoring to ensure that standards are maintained, and so it may negate the initial objectives of devolution and local accountability.

For these reasons the changes will not necessarily lead to immediate reductions in unit costs. Firms which seek to use restructuring simply as a public rationalisation for job-cutting to improve short-term profits are unlikely to achieve their objective, and at best will find that it is no better than a short-term palliative. The restructuring must be undertaken as an integral part of the firm's strategy. Its primary objective should be to increase flexibility and to make the organisation more responsive to the needs of the market, but it will not be effective in the long run if the strategy is not adapted to take advantage of these new characteristics.

Partly for these reasons, and particularly because of the reciprocal loyalty between employers and employees which offers lifelong employment in exchange for lifelong commitment and loyalty, Japanese firms have been reluctant to follow Western ideas of restructuring. The relative stagnation of the Japanese economy which started at the beginning of the 1990s led to tighter trading conditions and revealed substantial under-employment among white-collar employees. But there were no crash programmes of delayering. Cost-cutting measures included early retirement, reduced recruitment, cuts in bonus and overtime payments and transfers to affiliated companies. Large-scale layoffs were avoided in an attempt to maintain the implicit contracts between firms and employees (Lasserre and Schütte, 1995, especially pp. 94–5).

Corporate Memory

Even in Western economies where the emphasis on lifetime employment is not so strong, it is increasingly recognised that delayering may remove muscle as well as fat. Hierarchies may act as partially blocked filters but the members of staff may also be an important source of corporate memory which will be lost if the restructuring is pursued carelessly and insensitively. This may have important effects at both the operational and the strategic levels in the organisation.

Operational

At the operational level it may affect the organisation's ability to absorb minor irritations. Most cinema-goers will recognise that almost any film which involves an old steam engine will include a scene when the engineer has to hit one of the pipes with a spanner to ensure that the whole thing does not grind to a halt. Only the engineer knows for certain which pipe to hit. Large firms are generally more complex than steam engines but the same principles apply – they still require a good belt with a metaphorical spanner every now and then to keep them running smoothly. The middle managers in the middle of the hierarchy are often those who know where the pressure is needed – they know the way through the internal bureaucracy; they know the idiosyncrasies of suppliers and what to do if supplies are interrupted; and they know the best way to approach particular customers and how to identify those whose complaints may not be genuine. The knowledge is rarely transmittable through a company handbook: it is tacit knowledge which has to be accumulated rather than explicit knowledge which can be taught. There are things which can be done to preserve implicit knowledge, such as the use of Quality Circles or ensuring that new recruits work closely with more experienced workers in order to ensure that experience can be passed on. But it requires considerable care to ensure that implicit knowledge is not lost during a programme of restructuring.

Strategic

At the strategic level, the danger is that the partial destruction of corporate memory may erode the organisation's core competencies. The ideal core competencies are those which cannot be reproduced by competitors, and one of the most effective forms of security is the knowledge that reproduction will inevitably take a long time. Corporate learning which identifies the contacts which are most effective in ensuring that networks operate smoothly, or which develops the collective skills to ensure that a new development can be brought to fruition six or even three months earlier than competitors can achieve, for example, is a competency which cannot be reproduced at short notice although it can be destroyed all too easily by careless delayering or downsizing. In general, strategies must be designed to build on core competencies: restructuring must not destroy them.

Co-ordination

A further potential conflict between restructuring and strategic thinking may arise as and when it becomes necessary to co-ordinate the activities that have been restructured. It is true that a 'lean' organisation can operate more flexibly with devolved authority for local decisions and continuous process or product improvements, but it is also true that a series of largely independent operating units may evolve by continuous innovation to produce wasteful duplication and/or to ignore potential savings which might be available through the standardisation of components or the cross-fertilisation of ideas. Chandler (1990a) in particular, has argued that hierarchical structures are essential for the co-ordination that is needed if a firm is to realise the full potential of any economies of scale or scope. He suggested that during the early and middle decades of the twentieth century, Britain's tendency to rely on more personal and less hierarchical structures prevented British enterprises from becoming fully competitive with those of America or Germany. Since then the market pressures for variety and flexibility have introduced additional criteria for competitive success, but some co-ordination is still needed to ensure that devolved organisations do not fragment into distinct units following divergent or contradictory paths.

In particular, an emphasis on incremental improvements may overlook the substantial planning which is needed for the next generation of products and/or for new markets. It provides flexibility to respond to existing customers and existing competitors but does little to identify and prepare for future opportunities. These opportunities should not be conditioned by existing organisational arrangements but should reflect the competencies of the organisation as a whole – not just the business or operating units which may be the optimum focus for short-term flexibility.

It is therefore clear that there is a potential conflict between operational flexibility and strategic development based on the exploitation of core competencies. The devolved operating units must be balanced by a co-ordinating infrastructure, the first concentrating on immediate responses and gradual improvements while the second is concerned with links between operating units and with step jumps in development. We return to this tension in Chapter 6.

SMALL FIRMS – CHARACTERISTICS

Given the tension between flexibility and scale which exists in larger firms, it is now appropriate to consider the potential strengths and weaknesses of smaller firms, and the way in which these may impact on strategy.

Size and Scale

Size is relative. If you are a sole trader doing subcontract work in the building industry, a firm with twenty or thirty permanent employees will seem to be large. On the other hand, from the perspective of Royal-Dutch Shell a company like ICI may seem small. For statistical purposes the conventions generally put a dividing line somewhere between five and fifty employees to distinguish between small and medium-sized firms, and between 50 and 500 employees between medium and large firms, with the dividing line generally taken at lower levels in the service sector than in manufacturing industry. For competitive purposes, on the other hand, it will be more appropriate to take a relative measure of size based upon the existing dispersion of firm sizes within each industry. From this perspective firms will be small if they are substantially smaller than other firms in the same industry regardless of their absolute size.

Firms which are absolutely small will inevitably have fewer resources than large firms, but they are unlikely to be simply miniature versions of large firms because they will focus on a narrower range of activities. They may offer fewer distinct products or services ('horizontal specialisation'), they may undertake fewer processes ('vertical specialisation') or they may produce distinct products which are demanded in smaller quantities ('niche specialisation'). Hence while the absolute value of their resources will be smaller, the resources they devote to any particular product or process will be greater in proportion to their size than in larger firms. Differences between firms in the degree to which they are able to exploit economies of scale for particular products or processes may therefore be less than might be suggested by a simple comparison of their sizes. Differential economies of scope (marketing, finance, and so on) may be more significant.

Diversity

Small firms as a class are also very diverse and this diversity may not be competed away by market pressures. The diversity reflects the greater influence that a single entrepreneur may have in a smaller firm, and the variety of backgrounds, motives and goals which characterise the entrepreneurs. Some may seek self-employment for its own sake, and be determined to be their own boss in whatever line of business they chance upon; others may see it as the most effective way to get their own ideas off the drawing board and will be interested only in the development of those ideas; some may be 'refugees' who have been made redundant by larger firms and who turn to self employment almost as a last resort; and an increasing number of others may have accepted independence from larger firms to take over activities which are no longer part of the firms' core activities. In turn their different origins will be reflected in the firms' behaviour: some will focus on technical expertise and innovation, some may have management skills or market contacts to exploit, and some may only be interested in survival.

This diversity may persist for long periods because although small firms may face very intense market pressure, they do not necessarily face the same compulsion to conform as the large firms do (for an extended discussion, see Nooteboom, 1994).

Features which may encourage the continuation of diversity include:

- *Idiosyncratic sources of finance* – Increasingly large firms which use international sources of finance are forced to use common accounting conventions and face similar financial constraints, whereas smaller firms may tap a greater range of local sources with varied characteristics. Sometimes these may be private sources which offer finance on very favourable terms but in highly inelastic supply, so that the recipient may be very competitive but still unable to expand.
- *Risk myopia* – Some small firms may not be aware of, or may choose to ignore risks which might deter others. Some of these firms will succeed even if many fail.
- *More lenient regulations* – In many cases government regulations may exempt smaller firms. Even if they do not, the regulations may be more difficult to enforce against small firms because of their large numbers and more anonymous positions.
- *Toleration of low income* – Self-employed or family firms may struggle to preserve independence at income levels that would not be tolerated by a unionised work force and, by failing to distinguish between salary and profit, they may end up with a substandard return to the combined inputs of labour and capital.

Risk of Failure

Although many small firms are successful the risks of failure are high. The survival rate for new firms in the United Kingdom is reckoned to be no more than 30–50 per cent. The ratio is generally higher in South European countries such as Italy, where networking among small firms is more important. New firms there are more likely to be started to meet identified needs within a chain of suppliers and the new starter is likely to take its place immediately within a network of local enterprises and to focus on a specific area of expertise. The chances of survival may also be increased by prior experience of management. For example, American venture capitalists are more likely than their British counterparts to support new start-ups with an unproved product or market, partly because the American innovators are more likely to have spent some time in a larger corporation before they try to start up on their own. The experience may mean that they are both more practised in the art of management and more realistic about the factors which determine success or failure. This suggests that start-ups are more likely to succeed if they can slot directly into an established supply chain and if the starters have prior business experience.

Agglomeration

Small firms may be able to take advantage of the effects of agglomeration, which occur when firms of a similar type congregate in the same location. They may then find that they benefit from enhanced skills encouraged by the division of labour among interconnected units which may each focus on a specific task within the overall process of production. Innovation may be accelerated by the diversity of possible solutions which are tested by a number of independent but interconnected firms. The different firms may share suppliers and through subcontracting or referral of enquiries they may work together to meet unexpected surges in demand and so preserve customer loyalty. They may also benefit from a labour supply with appropriate skills for the work in question, and from the provision of specialist finance and other services, while buyers may be attracted by the number of options which are available to them in a small area, as commercial buyers of cheap toys are attracted to the numerous suppliers in downtown Los Angeles.

In the United Kingdom a survey of firms with fewer than 500 employees in the Cambridge area by Pratten (1991) suggested that agglomeration effects were important for relatively few firms and were not generally significant. But this is in contrast to American experience in areas like the Silicon Valley, with its focus on high-tech firms specialising in microprocessors, software and communications, who are linked by a variety of informal and formal co-operative practices, and an entrepreneurial culture which encourages openness, risk-seeking and a toleration of both independence and failure (Saxenian, 1994). It is also at variance with the resurgence of regional groupings of small interdependent firms in central and north-eastern Italy, which includes machinery and machine tools in Bologna and Modena, knitwear in Carpi, textiles in Prato, ceramics in Sassuolo and furniture or shoes in the Marche (Amin, 1989); and with the experience in Baden-Württemburg in Germany, where there is a mix of small and medium-sized makers of machine tools, textile equipment and automobile components.

SMALL FIRMS – STRATEGIC CONSIDERATIONS

Strategic Advantages

Clearly the strategy of a small firm will be constrained by its resource base, and it must seek to exploit any relative advantages it has by virtue of its size.

The diversity of small firms makes it difficult to generalise but it is still possible to identify some characteristics which are common to most if not all small firms and which may impact on their strategic development. The impact will be greatest when large and small firms coexist, either because the industry is in a state of transition or because it allows the simultaneous existence of more than one strategic group. On the other hand, the strategic significance of small size for the individual firm will be less when it is competing with other firms of the same size. This will generally be true in industries like furniture or clothing or domestic repair services where most firms are small and there are no significant economies of scale.

It is necessary to distinguish between those advantages which enable small firms to survive on the fringes of their industry and those which enable some firms to flourish and grow. The first category will include those circumstances which keep the prices of inputs down below their normal levels, so long as the firm continues to operate on a small scale. A small firm may work from low-cost premises such as a lockup workshop or a garden shed, as Hewlett and Packard did when they first set up to make electronic measuring equipment in 1938. The simplicity is an advantage while the firm remains small but is unlikely to accommodate significant growth nor is it necessarily an attractive condition for survival if low cost means inferior as well as small. This category will also include those idiosyncratic sources of capital which are in inelastic supply and may help to protect particular small firms without providing them with a basis for sustained growth. Firms which seek to grow will not normally find that finance is a limitation provided that they have a proven track record, but they may lose some degrees of freedom as they turn to more conventional sources of finance. Similarly a small firm may be able to exploit family labour for long hours at low wages and to set working conditions which are inferior to the norms in larger organisations, but may nevertheless be forced to improve conditions as it expands in order to attract a reasonable supply of skilled labour. Characteristics of this type may therefore aid survival but offer no basis for strategic development.

What we might call the strategic advantages of small firms fall under three headings: entrepreneurship, flexibility and contacts.

Entrepreneurship

Entrepreneurial talent is scarce. Individual entrepreneurs may often enjoy the relative freedom from bureaucratic control which they find in small firms, while at the same time their skill will have relatively more impact on performance because it can be applied directly and is not dissipated across a range of activities. The particular skills and interests of the entrepreneur will often dictate the strategic initiatives which are appropriate and any attempt to frustrate that choice would be counterproductive: initially the idea and an overriding commitment to the product or service concept may be more important than a detailed assessment of 'the bottom line'. The idea may not succeed, but it will certainly not succeed if it is tied down by bureaucracy before it has started.

Any initial success may be sustained if the entrepreneur is also a skilled manager. Many fortunes have been made in this way, but the attributes do not necessarily go together and it may be that the talents of the entrepreneur will need to be complemented by more routine management and administrative skills as the firm increases in size and scope. This transition is not easy, but the firm may fail if the individuals cannot accept that entrepreneurial flair must be adapted to satisfy financial constraints and the reality of the market.

Flexibility

Small firms have less complex organisational structures with more direct contact between 'the boss' and 'the shop floor'. This enables them to handle small volumes at relatively low cost and also gives them a more rapid response to change and a flexibility to meet the varied demands of customers. Some firms may still be dogged by resistance to change, but it is then a matter of will rather than structure, and even in craft-based trades where the preservation of old skills is important, the skilled craftsman can show great ingenuity in response to particular problems.

Close Contacts

Small size facilitates closer contact between managers and workers and also between all members of the firm and their customers or suppliers. As well as providing for flexibility such contacts may also make for increased trust so that the parties to any transaction, whether for employment or for the supply of goods and services, are less likely to insist on formal contractual arrangements and more ready to depend on mutual understanding. A greater use of implicit contracts may then reduce overall transaction costs by lowering the time and money spent in negotiating and recording each transaction. (Such differences can be significant. Although not related to size, it is notable that America, which generally relies less on implicit contracting than Japan, has 30 times more licensed lawyers for only twice the population (see Kester, 1991, p. 63).

The characteristics of entrepreneurship, flexibility and close contacts may enable smaller firms to respond readily to the growing demands of flexible markets, especially in service trades or in those manufacturing industries which offer a bespoke service. As we have seen, many large firms have used re-engineering, delayering and lean production in an attempt to increase their own flexibility. During the transition period, while large firms struggled to respond, small firms enjoyed a resurgence in many areas. This resurgence becomes more difficult to sustain without careful positioning as larger firms complete their restructuring, but small firms will continue to find it easier to compete in markets which are characterised by diverse, variable demands than they did when demand was satisfied by the mass production of standardised commodities.

Minimising Disadvantages

The main disadvantage of being small is in selling and marketing, especially overseas (Pratten, 1991). This is partly because a sales network which is needed to cover a large area and a promotional campaign which is aimed at the mass market will both have significant indivisible elements whose costs must be a deterrent unless they can be spread over a large output. Large firms may also be more credible to potential customers and be perceived as being more stable, although the latter may also depend partly on age and not on size alone. The credibility may be especially important for purchasers who are not able to judge the quality of a product for themselves before they buy, and the perceived stability may be important for purchases which involve a continuing relationship for repeat purchases or after-sales service.

For these reasons small firms may be most disadvantaged when selling at arm's length to the general public. In manufacturing, they may be less disadvantaged if they can concentrate on industrial markets which are technically sophisticated, because in these markets advertising will be less important and, since buyers are few in number, potential customers can be identified and contacted individually. A small firm may therefore be able to minimise the disadvantages if it acts as a supplier to other firms and offers capital goods, materials, consumables, components for further processing or assembly, or items which are to be distributed by the purchaser.

Outcomes

Some small firms may achieve the escape velocity which carries them clear of the gravitational pull of small size. The American firms Microsoft and Compaq are perhaps the best-known examples of explosive, sustained growth which was based on quality innovations which initially tapped a large domestic market. Many small firms, however, depend upon a niche market for their survival and this may inhibit their growth in the long run, especially if the niche is part of a relatively small national market.

An example of the protection afforded by niche markets occurs among the United Kingdom merchant banks, which are broadly equivalent to the American investment banks. Recent trends towards global competition and the wider dissemination of financial information have reduced the margins on their traditional business of financial intermediation and called for larger resources and stature than the traditional merchant banks had achieved or thought to be necessary. Several then lost their independence through acquisition by larger banks – Kleinwort Benson by Dresdner Bank, Morgan Grenfell by Deutsche Bank and SG Warburg by the Swiss Bank Corporation. The remaining independent merchant banks rely heavily on niche strategies. For example, Rothschild has strength in gold bullion trading and as a specialist adviser for privatisation.

However, as we saw in Chapter 2 (page 34), while niche markets may aid entry or survival, a firm may still be dangerously exposed if it seeks to move out of its niche towards the mass market. If it is to continue to grow, a small firm must either accept the fact of increasingly direct competition or it must sell out to a larger partner who has the greater stature needed to exploit their special skills. For example, the sale option was chosen in 1995 by Sonix, a firm which was founded in the United Kingdom in 1992 to produce internet-working devices which enable telephone networks to send and access computer information. The first year sales were more than quadrupled in four years but Sonix felt that its expansion was restricted and it then accepted an offer from 3Com, a computer networking company based in California with a turnover twenty times greater than Sonix. Through the deal Sonix effectively gained a worldwide sales force with new opportunities in North America and Asia Pacific (Smith, 1996).

On the other hand, if it continues to grow independently a firm must eventually accept the fact that its niche markets will no longer offer it effective protection. This was part of the experience of Amstrad, which dominated the United Kingdom market for consumer electronics during the 1980s. Initially the company's early success in home electronics carried over to assist its early entry into the computer market with the Amstrad PCW word-processor in 1985. The product was not technically advanced but it offered a user-friendly system for unsophisticated buyers who had no interest in further refinements nor in networking. It was followed successfully by an IBM-compatible p.c. in 1986, but problems arose at the end of the 1980s when it attempted to enter the business market with the PC2000 range. The product suffered from component failures which eventually led to court action against suppliers, but Amstrad also faced mobility barriers as it tried to enter a more sophisticated market in which customers expected the high standards of service and support which they already received from established suppliers (West, 1992). The company continued to market electronic products based on innovative design but it could not recover its earlier strength and in 1997 it announced that it would break up and distribute assets to shareholders. The shareholders were to receive a distribution of cash, 'litigation vouchers' covering anticipated receipts from the outstanding legal claims, and shares in two separate companies: Betacom, a consumer electronics group, and Viglen Technology, which assembled and marketed personal computers through direct sales.

ll firms have different characteristics. Small firms have the
_ntages of entrepreneurship, flexibility and local contacts.
Large firms have greater absolute resources, may enjoy economies of scale,
and can more readily carry the indivisible elements in the costs of selling and
marketing, but they may struggle to achieve flexibility or to cope with small
and irregular items within an organisation which is designed to handle large
items on a repetitive basis. We have seen that small firms often survive as
suppliers to larger organisations in order to avoid the disadvantages they
face in selling and mass marketing, but in many cases large and small firms
may find that their complementary advantages can be exploited through
some form of collaborative relationship which goes beyond a simple
contract between buyer and seller.

This is quite common in retailing where franchising arrangements may
combine the brand name and buying power of a large franchiser with the
stronger motivation and local knowledge of small franchisees. McDonald's
is a leading example. Similarly, small computer sales and service groups may
be able to reduce risk through close relationships and collaborative marketing with large suppliers such as Intel or Microsoft while simultaneously
acting as a source of information on local developments.

Occasionally the relationships between large and small firms may develop
into something approaching a market sharing agreement in which the firms
collaborate to ensure full market coverage while simultaneously focusing on
the market segments to which their size is most suited. This sort of
arrangement underlies the relationship between British Airways and its
eight franchise partners, of which the largest is Manx Airlines. This smaller
airline was established primarily to serve the local needs of the Isle of Man,
which is a small island at the geographical centre of the British Isles between
England and Ireland, with a population of approximately 75,000. The
airline now flies a large proportion of its network under a franchise
agreement with British Airways (BA) under the brand name of British
Airways Express. Manx Airlines carries all the commercial risk and pays
fees for the use of the brand and for services provided in reservations,
accounting and so on. Aircraft operate in BA livery and the crew wear BA
uniforms.

Clearly the primary focus of BA is on international flights using major
airports and large aircraft to handle large numbers of passengers. On the
other hand Manx Airlines has experience as a regional airline which makes
it better equipped to operate short-haul aircraft from smaller airports and
often with a different clientele. The franchising arrangement allows BA to
focus on its strengths while maintaining an identity in regional markets and
generating traffic for its long-haul services from the feeder services which are
operated by the franchisees. In turn the franchisees gain from the marketing

power of the bigger brand – Manx Airlines found it difficult to develop the Southampton/Brussels route under its own name but has had more success on the same route flying as British Airways Express. Franchisees may also gain business ceded to them by the franchiser – recently BA pulled out of six short-haul routes in Scotland carrying over 6,000 passengers a year in favour of their operation by Manx Airlines as a franchised partner.

Arrangements of this nature can be quite stable and persist for some years, provided that both parties recognise the mutual benefits. This is not simply a matter of temporary advantage. If the arrangement is to last, both must recognise that there is no threat by the other to their core business, and the larger partner must acknowledge that the smaller partner has particular skills which would not survive if the two firms were to merge under a single control or if the smaller firm were driven out of the industry by the weight of competition. If these conditions are not met, smaller firms may choose consciously to avoid collaboration in order to preserve their identity. In the past this has been particularly true of small firms in South Korea, where the earlier political decision to concentrate resources on a small group of firms which were given cheap credit and protection from foreign competition has been followed by rapid growth but has led to an economy dominated by a small number of giant *chaebol*. Small firms may then depend solely on a *chaebol* for sales but, unlike in Japan, will probably not be fostered by their giant neighbours. Some small firms, like Korea Biotech, chose to avoid the *chaebol* and market directly to universities or independent laboratories. Others, like the 15 leathergoods manufacturers covered by the brand name Capacci, have chosen a co-operative venture to share marketing costs (*The Economist*, 6 July 1996).

4 Supply Chain Co-ordination

INTRODUCTION

This chapter looks at the strategic implications of particular questions about procurement and distribution: namely, whether other firms should be paid to provide the goods and services required or whether they should be provided in-house. The chapter first describes the main issues, and then turns to a fairly abstract discussion of the nature of the choices involved, using the perspective of transaction cost theory. This is then used to underpin a critical look at the decline of in-house provision which has been common during the last two decades of the twentieth century, in a section which also considers the strength of some of the claims which are made from time to time to justify in-house provision. Finally the chapter turns to outsourcing, or market procurement, to re-emphasise the strategic significance of some decisions.

THE MAIN ISSUES

The Nature of Supply Chains

A supply chain links together the various stages which are involved in providing products or services for consumption or final use. For manufacturing goods the chain will stretch from the initial manufacture and production of materials through various intermediate stages for components or semi-finished products, and through final manufacture or assembly along various distribution channels to the final user. Services chains are often simpler and shorter, but items such as some financial or media services may pass through several steps in the distribution channel, and even the simplest personal services such as those provided by a self-employed hairdresser will require inputs of shampoos, lotions, towels and other consumables. Porter (1985) refers to the totality surrounding one firm as the 'value chain', partly to emphasise that each step is justified only if it creates more in value to the end user than it consumes as cost, and partly to emphasise that an individual firm's competitive position depends upon the effectiveness of the chain as a whole and not just on its own position as a link in that chain.

The supply chain must be co-ordinated in some way. This may be done by the market mechanism, when each firm in the chain concentrates on a single separable stage in the process and relies on purchases from other firms or sales to other firms to provide the necessary linkages between stages. We will refer to this as market co-ordination, and to the individual firm's action as outsourcing. Alternatively some firms may seek to combine two or more stages under a single control, and rely upon internal management to ensure co-ordination. Such action is referred to as vertical integration. Between these two extremes we may find many hybrid cases where one firm acts as a contractor to co-ordinate the other links in the chain but relies upon external agreements rather than internal management, as Benetton does in a section of the clothing industry. Benetton is a clothing services company rather than a manufacturer or retailer, although its branded goods are sold in over 100 countries through some 7,000 shops which use the Benetton brand name. In fact the shops are owned by independents who are customers of Benetton: they pay no royalties and carry all the risks of their stockholding. Similarly much of the manufacturing is contracted out to independent suppliers and the company will only undertake processing in-house when these are thought to be crucial for quality and cost effectiveness, as may be the case with design, dyeing and packaging. The system is co-ordinated by Benetton through contracts with suppliers or retailers, aided by agents who liaise with retailers and feed back market information to the company.

Depth and Breadth of Integration

Firms which seek to combine more than one link in the chain through vertical integration may choose a number of alternative dimensions. They may vary the breadth, relying on market co-ordination for some activities while integrating others, just as Benetton retain in-house dyeing but rely on market/contractual means to co-ordinate the independent links in the chain. Alternatively they may vary the depth of their integration, possibly seeking to combine more than two stages in the process, as many oil companies do who cover the whole chain from exploration and extraction through refining to distribution, marketing and retailing. However, even the deepest vertical integration is never total. The oil companies rely on market co-ordination for supplies of capital equipment and consumables; they may use independent pipeline operators, shippers or hauliers for much of their transportation; and they frequently trade supplies of crude or refined products with one another in order to maintain the balance of their supply chain.

This hybrid system, in which firms rely on independents for part of their requirements of a product or service while providing the rest in-house, is common throughout industry. It is most obvious for manufacturers who retail their own products. In the United Kingdom, for example, brewers may sell most of their beer through owned or contractually 'tied' outlets but still sell substantial volumes through 'free' houses and off-licences. But in some form or another the hybrid system exists in a wide range of different contexts. For example, firms may seek to balance outsourcing and in-house provision for financial services or training or transportation, and even those which seek to internalise all their component or material supplies may need to turn to independent suppliers from time to time in order to cover a breakdown in production or to meet an unexpected surge in demand.

In some cases, in particular industries or particular countries, the normal alternative of market co-ordination may not be available because the existing sources of supply are inadequate and cannot develop quickly enough to provide a credible alternative to integration. Vertical integration may then be the only feasible option. In the United Kingdom this was true of the motor industry before the development of an effective light engineering industry in the 1920s and 1930s (Rhys, 1972) and of the attempts to establish a watch-manufacturing industry after the 1939–45 war (Edwards and Townsend, 1962). Similar considerations have influenced the integrated growth of the South Korean *chaebol* (Lasserre and Schütte, 1995). In most cases, however, a firm will have an open choice between outsourcing and integration, and for the remainder of this chapter we shall assume that such a choice exists. The choice may be made for strategic reasons and it will undoubtedly have strategic implications.

THE CHOICE: OUTSOURCING OR INTEGRATION?

The Trade-Off

Outsourcing will generally offer the advantages of specialisation. Independent agents may develop specialised skills for the products or services they offer; they may exploit economies of scale by providing simultaneously for the needs of several users; and they may be subject to market incentives to efficiency which are more effective than internal control mechanisms. By contrast, integrated production will be less efficient unless the firm can match the scale and competency of the independent suppliers, and it may also impose opportunity costs if it absorbs limited resources which might otherwise be used for more profitable ventures. For these reasons it is always sensible to start with an assumption that a firm ought to be able to buy from an independent supplier at prices which are below the alternative cost of internal, integrated production, unless there is good evidence to the contrary.

On the other hand, any use of the market to obtain supplies of components and materials or outlets for the finished product will involve transaction costs. These will include such things as the cost of assessing the value of the product or service and the cost of maintaining agreements, through policing and enforcement if necessary. Some of these costs will involve separate purchases, such as the cost of legal services; some will involve clear internal costs of administration, such as the arrangements for ordering and payment; but the transaction costs will also include items which may not be included in direct costing such as the time taken to acquire information or the risk of loss if something goes wrong. If these transaction costs are too high they may offset the advantages of specialisation and indicate that vertical integration may be preferable to outsourcing.

The analysis of transaction costs as a motive for integration originates with Coase (1937), and owes much to subsequent development by Williamson (1975, 1985). North (1990) has given a lucid analysis of the relationship between transaction costs and institutions, or 'the rules of the game'. The analysis does not describe the thought processes of individual managers, whose motives will normally be expressed in less abstract language, but it does help to explain why integration takes place and why the motives may change from to time. The operational motives quoted by business managers and analysts may then be reviewed in the light of this general explanation.

Transaction Costs

A transaction may be divided roughly into three stages: search, negotiation and implementation. It will be convenient to consider these stages separately, although in practice specific elements of the costs may overlap two or more stages.

Search

A transaction can only take place if the parties can identify each other. This should not be a problem in the case of routine purchases, but new requirements may need an extensive search to establish the identity and reliability of potential suppliers, and a new entrant to an unfamiliar market must be able to identify potential distribution channels for its product. In general, higher search costs may be expected to discourage outsourcing and increase the incentive for integration.

Search would be unnecessary if the firm started with perfect information, and the need to search will be reduced by anything which makes relevant information more readily available. This may be done by government agencies or by other bodies, and in general it is more likely if the market is fairly broad. The costs of searching may then be reduced by the sort of institutional arrangements which set terms and define standards in many commodity markets, for example, or by events like trade fairs which allow some assessment if not full appraisal of alternative suppliers. Similarly the costs may be reduced as purchases become more frequent: regular trading in a particular market will increase a firm's knowledge of that market and reduce the need for any additional searches.

The significance of search costs will also depend on the number of items required. If the transaction relates to items which are to be purchased frequently in large quantities, then the unit search cost will be lower because the total search costs will be fixed or will not rise in proportion to the total number of units. By contrast, the costs for a small, one-off requirement may be prohibitive or may allow, at best, a limited search which is less likely to produce reliable results. The balance of advantage is then shifted in favour of in-house provision. For example, it may sometimes be sensible to produce an experimental component in-house but to search for independent suppliers if the component goes into full production.

Negotiation

Routine trading may be based upon standard contracts which are recognised by both parties and do not need to be renegotiated for each purchase, but any transaction which is not routine will require a separate contract, and this has to be negotiated. The negotiations will absorb management time and involve expenditure on legal advice. More complex transactions will need more complex contracts to protect the rights of all parties and will therefore involve more costly negotiations. *Ceteris paribus*, a firm is more likely to internalise a complex transaction unless the costs are clearly offset by the benefits of market co-ordination. As we shall see, such considerations may often undermine strategic alliances (pages 156–7 below).

All negotiations will be conditioned by bounded rationality: that is , by the limited capacity of the human mind to comprehend, formulate and solve complex problems. This means that the negotiators cannot possibly foresee every contingency and cannot be sure that the monitoring and control will be tight enough to secure a reasonable outcome during the implementation of the contract. This uncertainty may be all that is needed to encourage integration in some cases. For example, when distinct processes are linked together physically for technological reasons, as in the production and early processing of steel where the processes are linked together to conserve heat, the stages are integrated under a single ownership because, with the best will in the world, it would be extremely difficult to draw up a contract which separated the operations between independent organisations. More generally, the greater is the uncertainty, or the fear that the contract will not cover all relevant contingencies, the more likely it is that the firm will prefer vertical integration which brings the unknown future problems under a single control.

In some cases, however, the negotiators may accept that some contingencies should be left out of the contract to be resolved as and when they occur. This is most likely in industries that have evolved formal rules and procedures for settling disputes, or where arrangements for arbitration have become part of established business practice. The parties may then be more ready to accept an incomplete contract, and this will cut down on the negotiating time and reduce transaction costs.

Implementation

Many contracts will be concluded to the satisfaction of both parties, but some will not. If one or other of the parties believes that an incomplete contract has resulted in a distortion away from their notion of an acceptable outcome they may seek to renegotiate the contract, and either of them may then seek to replace it with administrative control through integration. Further, the fear that this might happen may lead to a breakdown in negotiations, and a preference for integration, even before the contract is signed. In general, the consequences of any breakdown will depend in part on the extent to which any investment outlays are or are not recoverable if something goes wrong – a breakdown which encourages a buyer to switch to another supplier will be less traumatic than one which forces the buyer or seller to abandon unrecoverable investments.

A contract may break down because of a dispute over the monitoring of the outcome. Normally the contract should include any appropriate definitions of quality, and industries like construction which rely heavily on complex contracts have developed routine procedures for measuring standard work – although there may still be wide margins for dispute over non-standard items. In general, however, a transaction will be suspect if either party lacks a satisfactory way of measuring the outcome. The suspicion will be increased if imperfect monitoring leaves open the possibility of opportunistic behaviour by one of the parties, as, for example, when a casual market trader knows that he will be gone long before the customers notice the shoddiness of his goods, or when a cheap-jack retailer damages a manufacturer's reputation by failing to provide services which were supposed to be included as part of the transaction.

In these simple examples the scope for opportunism arises both because the monitoring is imperfect and because the transactions are unlikely to be repeated. In general, for simple transactions, there is less likelihood of opportunistic behaviour if both parties expect to gain if the transaction is repeated and becomes one of a series and/or if they are concerned to establish or protect a reputation for fair dealing. On the other hand some opportunistic behaviour may be inevitable in more complex transactions, especially those which require one or both of the parties to make investments whose value depends on the outcome of the transaction, and where bounded rationality during negotiations means that some of the gains that may be generated by the transaction cannot be included in the contract and have to be determined after the investments have been committed.

One example might be the joint development of a new component which is produced by one party and incorporated into a final product by the other party. The component may prove to enhance the product in unexpected ways, but its value will be very difficult to assess until the product has been sold, and the component supplier may then fear that the producer will try to appropriate all the gains which are not covered explicitly by the contract. The problem becomes more complex if the supplier has installed new equipment or perhaps built a new plant solely to supply the buyer. After the plant has been built the buyer may try to force down the price of the component, especially if the supplier has few other uses for the plant. Alternatively the supplier may be able to press for more favourable terms if it appears that the buyer has no alternative source of supply and could not easily tolerate any disruption in the supply of components. In practice, the fear of such opportunistic behaviour may be enough to undermine the transaction before it starts, and encourage one or other party to seek an integrated solution.

Further, if the contract does go ahead, the joint development may produce an increase in knowledge which could lead on to a whole new family of components with enhanced properties. Who owns these residual rights once the transaction has been completed? Unless the results were foreseen, they could not have been covered fully by the contract and both parties will have an incentive to maximise their share. Alternatively, in a joint venture of this kind, one of the parties may fear a leakage of information about matters which are not covered by the contract, and this may further increase their reluctance to use a market transaction for something which they might be able to do in-house.

Note, however, that if the two firms merge in an attempt to internalise all rights and leakages, their action will inevitably change the pattern of incentives which were previously perceived by the managers of the independent firms. By definition, the residual rights cannot be specified in advance and so the merger will change incentives and behaviour in unpredictable ways. What is certain is that the merger does not simply replace an incomplete contract with a perfect system of internal control (see especially Grossman and Hart, 1986).

Informal Constraints

The impossibility of specifying complete contracts may sometimes encourage integration, but this is not the only possible outcome. In other cases the imperfections may be partially offset by informal constraints which modify potentially opportunistic behaviour. These constraints may include the firm's concern for its reputation, their acceptance of the behavioural norms of society or of their profession, and their adoption of conventions that grow out of repetitive transactions (North, 1990, especially p. 61). In long-term trading relationships the parties may then depend upon mutual understanding and trust in preference to either integration or formal contracts. The implicit contracts that result may work more smoothly and be adjusted more quickly, at less cost, than formal contracts, and may retain the advantages of specialisation and incentives which may come from market co-ordination. Implicit contracts may also enable disputes to be settled more readily without recourse to the courts or to formal arbitration.

In the past it has generally been true that trading relationships within Japan have made much more extensive use of implicit contracts than have comparable Western firms. The implicit contracts in Japan have been aided by social norms which militate against opportunistic behaviour, reinforced by reciprocal shareholdings between firms, extensive informal networks for information, management continuity and a readiness by major equity owning stakeholders like the banks to intervene selectively before problems and disputes become insurmountable.

These relationships may be changing. Many Western firms have come to accept the advantages of implicit contracting and, for example, Saxenian (1994) observed that the practice had been common for some time in Silicon Valley where geographical proximity promotes interaction and trust between firms and encourages collaboration. On the other hand, some Japanese firms appear to have been more ready to break longstanding relationships in the face of commercial pressures during a recession, and it must not be assumed that implicit contracting can resolve all the problems of market transactions. It may imply increased search costs until and unless all relevant partners become trusted collaborators; and although it eliminates negotiation and provides informal means to resolve unforeseen contingencies, it cannot remove the issue of residual rights and so it leaves open the incentives for opportunistic behaviour. Even when the formal rules are changed, the informal constraints set by custom or traditional codes of conduct are likely to be more inflexible and to delay changes in established practices.

Summary

It may be appropriate to summarise the main points of this section before going on to consider the practical implications. The discussion of transaction costs suggests that market co-ordination is most effective when goods and services are standardised or at least well understood, are frequently traded and are available from several suppliers who in turn supply several customers and use assets which are not specific to individual buyers. In such conditions the individual transactions are readily separable from each other and transaction costs will be minimised.

Different conditions arise when the transaction involves clear interdependence between individual buyers and sellers, either because the product or service is specific to that relationship or because one party becomes locked in to the relationship by irreversible investments. The interdependence may then be seen to impose an unacceptable degree of risk: any contractual errors or omissions will be potentially more significant and may be compounded by opportunism. Some of these problems may be reduced by implicit contracting. Vertical integration remains as an extreme solution but it may be undermined by distorted incentives and inefficiency.

THE DECLINE OF VERTICAL INTEGRATION

General Changes

During the first phase of the development of strategic thinking, vertical integration was often ranked alongside economies of scale and experience as a major source of productive efficiency. At that time integration was encouraged by an overriding faith in the advantages of scale and scope coupled with a search for effective control as technocratic managers sought to secure supplies or outlets at predictable costs. It was probably also encouraged by statistical estimates of the relationship between integration and profitability which came from sources like the PIMS data base (Buzzell, 1983). The statistical measures of integration which were used were not always convincing, being based upon the participants own judgement of their relative position, coupled with the numerical ratio of value added to sales which may vary systematically between industries regardless of the separability of processes, and at best measures 'firms in integrated industries' rather than 'integrated firms'. Nevertheless the data did suggest that integration was associated positively with high returns on investment, and that the net effects were more favourable in large firms, provided that any gains in the profit margin on sales were not offset by disproportionate increases in capital intensity.

Changes came with the growing demand for variety and flexibility which led to the introduction of 'lean production' in Japan and its progressive adoption by manufacturing and service companies in other countries. Regardless of whether integration did actually contribute to lower costs and higher profits while demand was focused on standardised products, it undoubtedly became less and less effective as the demand for variety increased. The interconnected reasons for this change include:

- Changing market demand may upset the balance between processes. If the different processes have different cost characteristics which give different optimum sizes, a series of integrated processes can only be in perfect balance at a few discrete levels of output when the optima coincide. This may be no more than a minor problem so long as the production can be planned in advance and held close to that level. It becomes more of a problem if frequent changes are needed to meet market demands.
- Vertical integration will make for a higher capital intensity for the firm because more capital is required for the additional processes at the same

level of output. The higher intensity will generally increase the risks faced by the firm as demand becomes less predictable.

- Integrated facilities may be able to cover only a limited range of product specifications. Firms must therefore turn to outsourcing if the market calls for a greater range of styles or qualities than the firms can provide with their own facilities.
- The management capacity which is needed to co-ordinate the integrated processes may need to be diverted from other functions. This diversion becomes more critical if management as a whole has to become more responsive to meet frequent changes in demand. At the same time the manager of an integrated firm must be able to cover the diverse requirements of the different processes and this diversity becomes more time-consuming and may be less easy to comprehend as the balance changes.

For these reasons it is apparent that vertical integration may become less effective and more costly as a means of co-ordination when the demand for the final product becomes more variable and less standardised. This would be expected to encourage outsourcing so long as transaction costs do not increase simultaneously to offset the declining efficiency of integration. This offset might occur if the markets became completely unstable, but it seems unlikely. Frequent changes in the level and specification of demand will involve some increase in transaction costs, but in practice these increases may be contained by other developments. The risks posed by opportunistic behaviour are likely to be reduced by the greater use of general-purpose machinery which is not specific to any one transaction and therefore has a higher residual value in alternative uses, and also by the trend towards global competition which has accompanied the changes in demand and may constrain opportunism by providing a wider range of alternatives. Bounded rationality will undoubtedly become more critical as it becomes more difficult to foresee all future contingencies in unstable markets, but this may be partially offset by the general acceptance of shorter contract periods and it is undoubtedly offset in practice by the increased use of implicit contracting. Changes in transaction costs are therefore unlikely to offset the increased costs and risks of vertical integration.

Special Claims

Outsourcing and implicit contracting will be considered in the final section of this chapter (pages 78–82 below). First, however, it is worth looking at some of the other claims which may be made in defence of integration. In practice, just as the problems of vertical integration have become more significant, so it becomes apparent that some of these claims may be suspect or relegated to the level of special cases. They are not necessarily wrong, but they must be considered more critically than once seemed to be necessary. The claims relate to quality, innovation, entry and market leverage.

Quality Control

Vertical integration may be undertaken to improve the quality of suppliers or outlets when the independent operators are demonstrably inefficient. This condition may be found in some underdeveloped markets and/or in particular industries when technology is changing rapidly and is not widely understood. In general, however, it is likely to be offset by the competitive pressures for efficiency and the advantages of specialisation which are generally characteristic of firms in developed markets, and by the increased emphasis on quality assurance which is now a broadly accepted feature of operations in most organisations. Individual firms may justifiably claim superior quality for their own core operations but should not assume that this superiority extends to non-core activities which are in turn the specialised focus of their suppliers or distributors. If the quality and reliability are found to be suspect, it may be more sensible to assume that this is a temporary aberration rather than a structural defect: negotiation and advice are likely to be more profitable than integration.

This general rule may be applied fairly easily to sequential operations which are linked to but separable from the core business. It may be less clear when applied to support services because the division between core and non-core may then be less obvious. For example, it is generally recognised that support activities like catering and cleaning are not core activities for most firms and may readily be contracted out, but financial services may be less clear-cut. Few firms outside the financial services sector would claim that general financial services are part of their core business, and most of them may be outsourced through large accountancy or consultancy organisations. On the other hand some conglomerate firms may justifiably claim that superior financial management is one of the benefits which the centre can offer to its diverse subsidiaries, and most firms would see some aspects of financial analysis and interpretation as key management operations which cannot be contracted out. A useful guide might be that bean counting and routine number crunching may be outsourced, while financial operations should be kept in-house if they involve commercial judgement and/or have strategic implications.

Control of Innovation

Innovative firms are unlikely to follow a general strategy of vertical integration without more specific incentives, but it has been argued that integration provides a breadth of knowledge which may be useful to an innovator, and that it improves the co-ordination of marketing and technical functions which may be a critical requirement for effective innovation (Mansfield and Wagner, 1975).

The argument is most likely to be genuine if innovation is seen as a linear process. In such a process a new product is first developed or designed and the finished design is then passed on to the engineers who decide how it is to be made; the engineering specification is then passed on to the production staff who lay out the processes and arrange for supplies of components and materials; and the marketing people might then become involved at about the same time, or perhaps a little later. A design fault which comes to light at any stage might involve a complete recycle through the process, unless it is too late to change, in which case the producers and marketers would just have to make the best of a bad job.

This may sound like a parody, but systems like this were not uncommon when organisations were characterised by hierarchical and functional divisions, and integration might then have helped to ensure that potential constraints in engineering and production would be appreciated by the design team, or that marketers were aware of the products they would have to sell, and might even have had some influence on the design, before they were presented with a *fait accompli*. But integration becomes increasingly irrelevant if the firm adopts a more open style and replaces the sequential model with a team-based approach in which outsiders are involved at an early stage.

Open, team-based innovation probably originated in high-tech industries where firms accepted that they could not cover all aspects of the developing technology and therefore began to welcome suppliers as partners in a joint process of designing, developing and manufacturing innovative products. The approach began to spread rapidly after the early 1980s, and was probably adopted earlier in Japan than in America or Western Europe. It is often exemplified by Team Taurus (see especially Walton, 1989).

In 1980 Ford adopted a new design process for a new range of cars which became the Ford Taurus and Mercury Sable. The process, which became known as Team Taurus, established a Car Product Development Group with responsibility for overall direction, design and approval. The Group included engineering, manufacturing, service, purchasing, legal, sales and marketing staff from the outset: it therefore broke the conventional barriers between functions and replaced the old linear process by team work. Outsiders were called in to assist the Group at the earliest possible stage: independent distributors assisted the sales and marketing staff, insurance companies assisted the design staff, and selected suppliers became involved in both design and engineering. These suppliers were selected on the basis of the quality of their work. They were not given any guarantee of future contracts, although the successful ones did receive longer-term contracts than had been common under the old linear system. No empirical testing of the result was possible because there was no control group, but it is generally believed that the team approach helped to develop cars that were easier to make, had a better insurance rating and a more immediate customer appeal.

Open, team-based approaches which involve independent suppliers and distributors appear to undermine the claim that innovation can be managed more effectively in an integrated firm. Further, it appears that in some cases the inflexibility of integration can be positively harmful to innovation. Saxenian (1994) observed that when the American DEC (Digital Equipment Corporation) converted from minicomputers to personal computers it was hampered by vertical integration which left it with a narrow range of options and led to problems over timing and co-ordination. It will generally be impossible for any firm to remain at the leading edge of every relevant technology as the pace of innovation accelerates. DEC became locked into existing technologies and skills. By the early 1980s many of its internally manufactured components were technologically obsolete so that, for example, its disc drives were two years behind the best of its competitors.

The inclusion of independent suppliers at an early stage in new product development is now common, especially for complex assembled products like motor cars. For example, 'in 1995, more than 250 suppliers for the new 5 Series BMW had the opportunity to take part in the assembly of the components during prototype construction at the Dingolfing plant and thus to acquire know-how for their own production processes. In addition, before the start-up of the 5 Series, suppliers manufactured full production quality components in real time conditions and with the means at their disposal for series production. BMW experts provided the necessary support' (BMW Annual Report 1995). Note, in particular, that this report refers to established suppliers. It is clear that such co-operation will be facilitated by long term relationships which are based upon mutual respect and trust between buyer and seller, rather than by arm's length contractual relationships.

Entry Barriers

Vertical integration might possibly be expected to create entry barriers to protect quasi-monopolistic control of markets if it enables the integrated firm to secure effective control over scarce resources. It may also deter small entrants who may find it difficult to raise capital in imperfect markets, if it becomes necessary to enter the industry in an integrated mode. However, each of these alternatives needs to be treated with care and it is by no means as obvious as it might seem. In the first case (control of supply) it is the ownership of the resource which is critical. Integration may change the ownership of that resource but it does not create any additional barrier to entry. Indeed it may become a liability if the resource ceases to be an essential step in the value chain. In the second case (entry barriers) the integration will only be effective in raising the capital cost of entry if it also reduces unit costs or otherwise increases the effectiveness of operations. If there are no such advantages an unintegrated entrant will be able to obtain resources from independent suppliers at the same cost as the integrated firm, and the capital cost of integrated operations is not relevant to the entrant.

Examples of effective barriers do exist. In pharmaceuticals, for example, only the larger firms can afford the integration of marketing and production which is needed for the effective exploitation of profitable new products. Smaller firms are restricted to less profitable market segments or forced into some degree of dependency on larger firms. In general, however, attempts to create entry barriers through integration may not survive in the face of technical change and/or entry by established firms from other industries. The barriers may be more enduring if stagnation or slow growth inhibit new entry or technical progress, and integration may then be a more rational strategy, but any successes may prove to be short-lived if they attract the attention of the antitrust agencies.

As an example of the effects of technical change, consider the American film industry (Vogel, 1994). In the early 1970s the large film studios had what seemed to be an unassailable control of prices and distribution through their integrated ownership of cinemas. However, in the mid-1970s, Time Incorporated, then a major magazine publisher, set up Home Box Office as a separate organisation to handle movie distribution for pay television. The set-up costs were substantial but it succeeded in gaining what was effectively a monopoly buying role for cable television. The major studios did not react immediately, but by the 1980s they were seeking to re-establish control through a jointly owned pay channel, under the brand name of Premiere. But their position was further eroded by the growth of video cassette sales and alternative suppliers for pay television. Between 1980 and 1995 the proportion of film revenues generated by cinemas fell from more than one-half to about one-quarter. The threat of antitrust action together with disagreements over its operation led to the break-up of Premiere and the studios fell back on a series of separate defensive agreements with the independent cable companies.

Vertical integration was also thought to provide an effective entry barrier to the petroleum industry in the 1950s. World supplies of crude oil were then controlled by a few large firms who had integrated production and refining and then used their position to squeeze the margins obtainable by independent refiners. Later, however, in the 1960s the independents flourished as increased supplies of crude became available. It was clear that the entry barriers had depended solely on the control of scarce supplies of crude oil and that integration had had no additional effect (Adelman, 1972).

Similarly in the United Kingdom in the 1950s the outright purchase of many filling stations by the major oil companies, coupled with the solus tie system which bound independent retailers to specific companies, represented keen competition for market share among the established oil companies but seemed to be excluding new competitors. It undoubtedly helped to upgrade filling stations during a period of rapid expansion when the independent retailers might well have been held back by imperfect capital markets, but it could not profitably prevent the entry and expansion of either the full-price or the cut-price competitors when supplies became more readily available in the 1960s (Shaw and Sutton, 1976). Further, after the rapid cost increases and periodic supply shortages of the 1970s, the position of all the conventional suppliers was further undermined by the growth of petrol sales from filling stations attached to supermarkets. By the mid-1990s the supermarkets handled about one-quarter of all the petrol sales in the United Kingdom as their high volumes and shared facilities enabled them to keep down their operating costs and negotiate for lower prices from the suppliers. Similar conditions apply in France where the hyper-markets now supply about half of all retail sales of petrol, although the penetration of the large retail chains has been delayed by regulation in both Japan (which restricted imports of refined products until 1996) and Germany (where the cost conditions are affected by the limited shop-opening hours).

It must be accepted, however, that not all entry barriers will be eroded by technical change or by changes in supply conditions. Some may require a regulatory push. Until the late 1980s in the United Kingdom large quantities of draught beer were sold through 'tied houses' which were owned by the brewers and either staffed by their employees or leased to tenants who were allowed to stock only the beers which were nominated by the brewers. Given that sales through public houses represented a major part of total beer consumption, and that the number of public houses was restricted by the licensing authorities, the 'tied house' system constituted an effective barrier against independent brewers who sought to achieve any significant sales volume. In 1989, however, the Monopolies and Mergers Commission criticised the 'tied house' system and forced the major brewers to sell off almost a third of their houses. The proportion of tied outlets fell from nearly 60 per cent in 1986 to just over 30 per cent in 1994, and the sale of outlets permitted the entry and growth of specialist groups which operated public houses but did not own breweries. The growth of these independents appears to have taken some market power away from the brewers and its timing is circumstantial evidence that entry had previously been impeded by the tied house system.

Market Leverage

Regardless of its long-run effects on entry, forward integration may enable firms to increase their market leverage. We saw in Chapter 3 that forward integration into marketing and distribution may be a very real economy of scale or scope for large firms, and we should also note that in particular cases integration may have a strategic role in encouraging the more rapid development of distribution systems to meet new requirements. The petroleum companies may not have created permanent barriers to entry by their exploitation of the solus tie arrangements in the 1950s but they did ensure that the growth of outlets for petrol kept pace with and did not inhibit the growth of car ownership. They were therefore able to ensure that any imperfections in the supply of capital or enterprise to petrol retailers did not restrict the growth of petrol sales.

Similar considerations lay behind Intel's decision to move downstream in the mid-1990s. Intel is the world's largest producer of semiconductors, focusing on high-value-added processors rather than on the bulk commodity products like memory chips. In 1993 it introduced the Pentium processor while many p.c. manufacturers felt that they had still not fully exploited the market potential of the 486 processors which had been introduced in 1989. Intel was concerned by the slow uptake of the Pentium chip. It started to market the Pentium brand directly to consumers without reference to the p.c. manufacturers, and it also began to produce its own computer motherboards incorporating the Pentium processor. It subsequently scaled back its production of motherboards once the manufacturers had accepted its leverage and the demand for the new processors had been firmly established.

Intel's forward integration was clearly designed to influence but not to control the p.c. market, and it did not contradict the firm's clear strategic focus on processors. In other cases integration may change the strategic focus in ways which were not really intended and may be misunderstood. For example, partial forward integration may offend customers who are reluctant to buy from a competitor, as Baxter International found in the American health-care market when its attempts to distribute supplies through its own clinics conflicted with its established status as a distributor to hospitals (Sadtler *et al.*, 1997). A strategy of partial forward integration must always be considered very carefully unless the integrated and unintegrated sales are directed at different markets or market niches and/or partial integration is already established as a characteristic of the industry.

Further, a manufacturing firm which integrates forward into distribution in order to promote the sales of manufactured products may find as the competition intensifies that it has to focus more strongly on distribution in order to protect its investment in what was intended to be a minor activity. In general any such integration which is not intended to create a new core activity, can be justified more easily if the exit costs are fairly low so that the integration can be reversed or modified once its immediate objectives have been achieved.

Once again the oil industry provides an illustration. In the 1990s the industry came to be characterised by excess refining capacity and intense competition in product marketing, so that 'upstream' investment in exploration and production is generally more profitable than 'downstream' investment in refining and marketing. But the integrated companies find that divestment is not easy. Mergers may enable some to reduce duplication and economise on distribution facilities, as when British Petroleum and the American-based Mobil agreed to merge their downstream operations in Europe in 1996. Refining capacity is more difficult. It was possible for integrated firms to off-load some capacity to independents with lower overheads and a tolerance for lower margins, and, for example, both Exxon and British Petroleum sold some of their American refineries to the independent company, Tosco.

Alternatively, in spite of the surplus capacity, some state-owned production companies in the Middle East were still prepared to purchase refineries which could provide guaranteed long-term outlets for their product. In most cases, however, it was difficult for one firm to do anything to reduce refining capacity. Short-run marginal costs in refining are low and well below average cost so that refineries may be kept on stream even when prices fall well below 'normal' levels, and the nature of refining means that the closure and dismantling of a refinery will involve very high reclamation costs. In such conditions the exit costs are high and the firms may continue for some time in an integrated mode even though their preferred strategy might involve a stronger focus on 'upstream' activities.

OUTSOURCING

Limitations

The balance between integration and market co-ordination has changed substantially against integration. For example, firms with particularly strong brands may now outsource most of their production in order to concentrate on developing their brand, and manufacturers who once prided themselves on their integrated facilities will now focus on the co-ordination and assembly of outsourced components rather than on their production. The main objective in such cases is to outsource activities which are not part of the core competency of the organisation in order to take advantage of specialisation and of the incentives which are offered by market co-ordination, and to free resources which can then be devoted to those things which the organisation does best.

The danger, as with almost any apparently clear strategic guideline, is that managers will overreact and become guilty of 'blue skies' outsourcing. If this is to be avoided, it must be accepted that the objective is not to outsource anything that can be outsourced, but to outsource everything that ought to be outsourced. The basic principle is that goods and services may be outsourced unless they contribute to the firm's core competency. Conversely, those which give the firm a lasting competitive advantage should be retained. There are, however, two riders to this simple guideline. The first is that the principle of comparative advantage applies. The ultimate aim is to retain and develop those competencies which strengthen the firm's strategic position. Given that resources are limited, this means that the available resources should be directed to those areas which yield the greatest advantage, even if the result is that resources have to be withdrawn from other areas in which the advantage, although positive, is slight. The second rider is to emphasise the importance of future competencies. One possible danger of outsourcing is that it may cut the firm off from the development of new skills and give it a narrower base on which to build future competency. The objective must be to retain those sources of competency which are expected to provide a competitive edge in the opening up of new markets or industries, and not just in existing applications. The difficulty is to avoid retaining everything in the sort of attic or lumber room which you find in houses where people can never bring themselves to throw anything away in case it might come in handy.

Further, even among the goods and services which are outsourced, some will be of greater significance and demand more attention than others. This is shown in Figure 4.1, which is based loosely on ground-rules implemented by the American company, 3M (van de Vliet, 1996).

Figure 4.1 defines the status of outsourced supplies in terms of the impact which their quality and readily availability have on operations and the impact which their prices and terms have on profits. As a simple example of the difference between the impact on operations and the impact on profits, consider the inputs which are needed to keep a car on the road. Tyres do not normally have a major impact on the running costs, but a blow-out may stop the car completely if you do not carry a spare. They therefore have significant operational impact but low profit impact. On the other hand,

Significance for operations

		Low	High
Significance for profits	Low	Delegated, simplified systems	Long-term contracts, stockholding for security
	High	Short-term contracts with frequent review	Intensive relationships with suppliers

Figure 4.1   Outsourcing: relations with suppliers

petrol (gasoline) will have a significant impact on both mobility (operations) and cost (profit), whereas fluid for the screen-washer has less effect on either, but may still count as an essential purchase in the long run.

Transition from Integration to Outsourcing

The example of the petroleum industry (page 78) serves as a reminder that firms may not be able to respond instantaneously to a change in incentives. They must be convinced that the change will persist before they act and their reaction will be further delayed if there are substantial exit barriers. Heavy investment in plant may be difficult to recover. Potential independent suppliers may be reluctant to take over facilities which were designed to meet the requirements of a single user, and integrated subsidiary companies may be difficult to sell unless they have first proved their efficiency by competing for business in the open market. Further, if it is not possible to dispose of the facilities as a going concern the closure of the unit may involve redundancy or reclamation costs. The decision to close a plant or outlet will also face resistance from trades unions or local political interests. In 1996, for example, the American General Motors corporation gained grudging union acceptance for increased outsourcing after initial strike action at two brake factories at Dayton, Ohio; but in the same year in Germany, Opel and Volkswagen agreed to freeze or reverse proposals to outsource supplies of components. Their action was taken partly because they believed that standardisation of components could ensure their efficiency as integrated producers, but it also followed and probably reflected trade union pressure.

The unions' reaction is understandable and predictable, especially if the change in strategy involves redundancies or a substantial drop in the employees' perception of security, and they may also have a genuine concern to ensure that the firm preserves the skills which are embodied in its staff. The fears about working conditions may be justified in some cases: in 1993, for example, the European Union issued a directive to protect the rights of employees in certain cases where services were contracted out to independent firms, by ensuring that contractors could not take over the old staff to do the same job for less money. In many cases, however, the specialist agencies may be able to offer better terms and conditions. ISS, a European contract cleaning firm based in Denmark, seeks to ensure that its employees receive better pay and are more highly trained than their counterparts who work in-house for other firms (*The Economist*, 5 March 1994). Similarly Pitney Bowes Management Services, which was set up in the mid-1990s by the American mail equipment firm, Pitney Bowes, to take over the operation of mail rooms, records and other business support services on a contract basis, believes that it offers staff career prospects which do not exist in what are often seen as dead-end jobs in large firms (Lewis, 1996). These potential gains arise because the specialisation which is encouraged by outsourcing may offer potential benefits to both the buyer and the seller.

Strategic Implications

If the switch from integration to outsourcing is to be successful it must be recognised as a strategic decision and supported accordingly. The traditional job of many purchasing departments was simply to identify reliable sources of supply, issue orders and possibly to negotiate for lower prices even when this involved squeezing the suppliers' margins. By contrast, supply chain co-ordination requires sophisticated management to reduce costs and increase value throughout the chain, and this may require close co-operation between customers and suppliers.

Intensive, strategic relationships depend upon mutual trust and a recognition of interdependence by both purchasers and suppliers. The purchasers aim to enhance value by simultaneously reducing transaction costs and gaining the benefits of functional specialisation by suppliers. But the suppliers must also expect to gain from the relationship and this requires at least an implicit recognition that any cost savings will be shared and not appropriated by the buyers pressing for unreasonably low margins; a readiness by the buyer to act openly and to share forecasts and analyses; and an understanding that the buyer will reject the supplier only if there are real problems such as unacceptable quality or delivery, attempts at opportunistic behaviour, or a genuine competitive offer which the supplier cannot match.

It will not be possible for the buyer to maintain strategic relationships with large numbers of suppliers. For several years the Japanese have combined implicit contracting with adherence to a relatively small group of selected suppliers, and many Western firms are now following this example. The Ford corporation reduced the number of suppliers by more than 40 per cent in the early 1990s, and in the United Kingdom the Rover car company almost halved the number in six years. This concentration may put heavy demands on the suppliers to meet the buyers' requirements, and even in Japan some purchasers have become more ready to break long-standing ties with suppliers if the latter prove to be less than fully effective. Component suppliers in the international motor industry have been encouraged to pool their activities in order to provide a more comprehensive package to the assembly firms, as the German component supplier, Robert Bosch, with strength in electronics, merged with America's Allied Signal, which had strength in hydraulic systems; and in 1996 Ford were reported to be brokering mergers which would lead to more suppliers of international standing (*The Economist*, 8 June 1996).

If the co-ordination is to work effectively the interdependence must be fully recognised by all members of the supply chain. Intermediate suppliers

should be aware of the requirements of the end users: they should understand the trade logic and appreciate the pattern of needs which generates the
final demand; and they should be able to anticipate changes in end-user
requirements and hence be able to contribute to new product developments
which aim to meet those changes without waiting for a detailed specification
from the producer or assembler whom they are supplying. Further, at the
day-to-day level, they must be able to match the producer's speed of
reaction to market changes. This requires delegation. A lean producer
cannot fully exploit its leanness if it has to buy strategic inputs from
suppliers who retain hierarchical structures with unwieldy procedures. In
extreme cases the mismatch could justify vertical integration by the purchaser, or at least a meaningful threat of integration to encourage the
supplier to accept the need for change.

Virtual Firms

In an increasing number of cases the extensive use of outsourcing has led to
the development of what might be called 'virtual' firms, in which co-
ordination and possibly design become the core competency of the firm
which contracts out all other operations. Some motor manufacturing firms
approach this level and have become assemblers and systems integrators,
outsourcing an increasing number of items and encouraging suppliers to
provide complete subassemblies rather than separate components. 'Fabless
firms' with no fabrication plants will design microchips and contract out
production to foundries which do not have their own design teams. In air
passenger transport several small firms have started as 'virtual' airlines with
leased aircraft, outsourcing everything from training to routine maintenance, and replacing agency sales by telephone reservation systems which
may be staffed by independent operators who work solely on commission.
Examples include Britain's Easyjet and Italy's Air One.
    In all such cases, however, we must recognise that the co-ordinator will be
seen by consumers as the supplier, and will retain moral and legal responsibility for the quality and safety of the product or service. Virtual
companies retain real responsibilities and must ensure that their co-ordination is fully effective.

5 Specialisation and Diversification

INTRODUCTION

Diversification is another feature of strategic development which has become less fashionable during the last two decades of the twentieth century, and many firms have reduced their scope during this period. This chapter first considers the reason for this change, arguing that firms became over-diversified both because of their own actions and because the context has changed in ways which have generally reduced the optimum level of diversification. Nevertheless, diversification continues to be characteristic of many firms: the simultaneity of specialisation and diversity is confirmed by the experience of three firms – Rio Tinto, BP and Volvo – which have sought consciously to narrow their scope.

The remainder of the chapter therefore considers the continuing case for diversification. This is founded on an analysis of resources, balancing those of the firm against those needed for success. The balance is then developed in a characteristics/context analysis, first in terms of strengths and opportunities and then in relation to weaknesses and threats.

REDUCTIONS IN SCOPE

Excessive Diversity

The significance of changes away from diversification is shown by an American study which indicated that at least one-fifth and perhaps as many as one-half of the Fortune 500 firms reduced the scope of their diversification between 1981 and 1987, whereas the comparable figure was only about one per cent of such firms during the 1960s and 1970s (Markides, 1993). The scale of this change suggests that in the 1980s the changes in scope were much more than routine strategic adjustments, and this is generally confirmed by more detailed analysis. Several of the studies surveyed by Johnson (1996) found that firms were generally performing badly just before they reduced the scope of their operations, and Markides (1995) found that refocusing by over-diversified firms has often led to significant improvements in profitability. (Note that statistical measures may be difficult to interpret because neither 'refocusing' nor 'over-diversification' can be measured precisely. However, Markides used five alternative measures of each variable and found that the effect on performance was confirmed in all but one of the 25 combinations of alternative measures.)

An Optimum Level of Diversification

In spite of the changes, diversification is not necessarily a misguided strategy. It may lead to higher profits if it enables a firm to benefit from new opportunities or to gain economies of scope by combining products synergistically. It may also enable a firm to survive and grow beyond the constraints set by its original product range. But diversification will also require the firm to take on additional processes or to enter into more value chains and will therefore make management more complex. As diversification increases there must come a time when the managers, constrained by bounded rationality, cannot fully comprehend every feature of every additional activity they take on. They may also find that the skills they acquired from experience with their established products are less relevant and may even be positively misleading when applied to the new activities, and their problems may be further compounded if they receive information in a variety of different 'languages' or technical jargon which has been distorted by the imperfect tuning of a complex organisation. The managers may therefore lack the competence and capacity which they would need to maintain effective oversight of all aspects of the business, and the different business units may begin to drift apart.

Textbooks commonly draw organisation charts with no more than three of four separate divisions, but Chandler (1990a) observed that large American corporations which might have had ten different divisions in the 1930s, were typically operating with between 40 and 70 divisions by 1969. Under such conditions the head office cannot have an intimate, detailed, strategic appreciation of all the operating divisions. It may then alienate other staff by misguided meddling, and waste resources by trying to force distinct units to co-operate and conform. It will also be forced to allocate resources between competing uses solely on the basis of general financial information, because it is no longer able to make an informed strategic appraisal. It therefore has to adopt an allocative role which, at best, can be no better than that of an external financial market, but at worst may be distorted by political machinations between the competing divisions. The head office may therefore become a costly irrelevance, and any attempt to re-establish control can only cause further harm.

These problems will increase as the firm's activities become more and more diverse until at some point they more than offset any gains. Conceptually it may therefore be possible to think of an optimum level of diversification: a specialised firm may gain initially as it diversifies, but it must eventually reach a point at which further diversification is counterproductive because of the deteriorating quality and increasing burden of managerial control. In theory the firm should not diversify beyond this level, although the level is not immutable and some further diversification may still prove to be beneficial if the optimum level rises as managers become more experienced in the diverse needs of their complex organisation.

In practice, it will be impossible to measure the optimum. Nevertheless it will still be meaningful to speak of 'over-diversification', in the sense that the performance of the firm is harmed by its current level of diversification, and any under-performance of this kind will become more and more difficult to sustain as the firm's markets become increasingly competitive.

Growth Beyond the Optimum

Firms may adopt strategies which make them over-diversified. This may be done deliberately, or because the firms fail to recognise their limitations.

Deliberate Strategies

In some cases occasional over-diversification may be part of a deliberate strategy, and a firm may plan for future downscoping even as it acts to increase its scope. For example, some firms may specialise in buying under-performing firms in order to improve their performance and resell them, and so they may be regularly increasing and decreasing their level of diversification. More generally, in some firms occasional divestment might occur as part of a continuing growth strategy. Given the uncertainty which is associated with any new venture a firm may deliberately initiate more projects than it expects to maintain, and may then withdraw from those which prove to be relatively less successful when subjected to the test of the market. Even if the firm has not planned such action as part of its strategy, it may become the preferred option if some areas prove to be more profitable than expected and so increase the opportunity cost of capital or management resources which are devoted to other areas. The firm may then reduce its scope in order to provide the cash or other resources which are needed to meet strategies for continued expansion.

Misguided Strategies

Firms may also become over-diversified by mistake, especially if diversification is a discrete process which must be undertaken in large steps rather than by gradual increments, because it will then be more difficult to prejudge its implications. The possibility that mistakes will be made is likely to be reinforced in practice by managerial hubris and/or if managers pursue their own objectives without due regard for the consequences. Their freedom to do so will be greater when the firm's governance is weak, and any tendency to under assess new projects will be reinforced if the firm also appears to have surplus funds available for investment. The risk may therefore be greatest in mature industries where core activities generate more cash than is needed for reinvestment, and may be less if funds have to be obtained from a more critical capital market. At times, however, even the capital markets may give the wrong signals – for example, it might be argued that in the 1960s and 1970s the financial markets generally were too ready to support conglomerates and were unwilling or unable to discriminate between them effectively.

Environmental Changes

The adverse effects of over-diversification have been reinforced by environmental changes which have made such positions less tenable. The changes may also have lowered the optimum level of diversification, thus forcing firms to reduce their scope even if they did not previously seem to be over-diversified.

There are at least two such changes that occurred in the 1980s and 1990s. First, capital markets have generally become more effective as a result of deregulation, increased competition and the improvements in information which have come with better communications and higher standards of disclosure by firms. Previously it was possible to argue that large diversified firms were more efficient than the imperfect capital markets at allocating finance for investment (Williamson, 1975, especially pp. 146–8), but this view became less tenable as progressive improvements in capital markets coincided with the over-diversification of firms which was gradually undermining the effectiveness of internal allocations.

Secondly, globalisation and changes in consumers' tastes have increased environmental turbulence and uncertainty and so increased the problems of managing diverse businesses. The intensity of global competition has also had the long-run effect of eroding the slack which enabled over-diversified firms to survive. In economists' terms, firms have been forced to move closer to their production possibility frontiers and to reject policies which lead to X-inefficiency (for a formal discussion of X-inefficiency, see Leibenstein, 1966).

The combined effects of changes in competition and more effective capital markets have also undermined the strength of those conglomerates which based their success on financial expertise and/or on the acquisition and reorganisation of under-performing companies which had otherwise survived because of inadequate competitive constraints. Norman Ireland, the head of the British conglomerate BTR, which grew from its base as a manufacturer of rubber products through a series of mergers in the 1980s and early 1990s, observed in 1995 that there were fewer inefficient companies around for the conglomerates to exploit (Lorenz, 1995). Subsequently, in 1996 BTR announced the reversal of its acquisition-led strategy. It disposed of units which had accounted for nearly one-quarter of group sales and reorganised the remainder into four primary groups (automotive, power drives, process control and packaging) and three smaller ones in order to give a clearer focus. In the same year another British conglomerate, Hanson, announced that it was to break up its diverse activities into four separate companies (tobacco, energy, chemicals and building materials): it had enjoyed very rapid growth in the early 1980s based on numerous acquisitions but its shares had under-performed the London stock exchange for five years or more before the announcement of its break-up. Somewhat earlier, the American company, Beatrice, which had been a rising conglomerate star in the early 1980s, had become an under-performing company itself by 1986 and was then taken over and subsequently dismembered in a leveraged buyout (see, for example, Gaughan, 1991); and in 1995 the American conglomerate ITT broke up into three successor companies covering insurance, leisure, and a group of manufacturing operations under ITT Industries.

There are exceptions, such as the American General Electric Company, which appears to depend upon unique management and financial skills to hold together its blend of power generation and appliances, broadcasting and industrial products. But most remaining conglomerates now seek to develop clusters of similar businesses related by some critical factor in a highly decentralised mode. For example, in the United Kingdom the Virgin Group covers travel and tourism, media, retailing, financial services and consumer products. The Group is built around a single brand which connotes quality, innovation and enjoyment, and it is very highly decentralised with a number of separate companies operating with outside investment under a shared name and ethos. For example, Virgin Retail, which runs a chain of music and entertainment media shops, is 25 per cent owned by Virgin and 75 per cent by W.H.Smith, which also operates a separate chain of newsagents and bookshops; while Virgin Direct, which was set up in 1995 to provide personal financial services, is a 50:50 partnership between Virgin and the financial services group AMP.

THE CONTINUED SIGNIFICANCE OF DIVERSIFICATION

Changes in the optimum level of diversification will have affected different firms to different degrees and in different ways, but the overall effect has clearly been to move the goalposts to favour a stronger focus on specialisation, and this has led to extensive downscoping or de-diversification. But the changes do not eliminate the case for diversification as a component of business strategy, and the effects of downscoping on individual firms, although significant, should not be exaggerated.

Asia

Although refocusing is not solely a Western phenomenon, its intensity there has generally not been matched by firms in the Asia Pacific group of countries. Consider, for example, the South Korean *chaebol* which owed their initial success to the government's policy of forced industrialisation in the 1960s when it favoured a limited number of entrepreneurs with preferential credit, tax advantages and protection from imports. By 1993 the turnover of the four largest *chaebol* (Samsung, Hyundai, LG (formerly Lucky Goldstar) and Daewoo) was equivalent to approximately half of the national GNP, while the turnover of the largest thirty was equivalent to over 80 per cent (Lasserre and Schütte, 1995). All the *chaebol* are highly diversified. Hyundai, the second largest by turnover and the largest by asset value, promoted itself in 1996 as a 'global force in such diverse industries as automobiles, electronics, iron and steel, shipbuilding, engineering and construction, machinery and petrochemicals'. The Korean government has become concerned by the national dominance of the *chaebol* and the absence of a thriving small firm sector, and in 1993/4 it announced that financial support would in future be conditional on more focused attention to core businesses. There have since been some moves towards down-scoping. For example, Pohang Iron & Steel has sold some loss-making divisions, and LG's electronics subsidiary has disposed of two businesses and focused activities on four in place of ten business units (*The Economist*, 14 September 1996). The changes reflect competitive pressures as well as, if not more than, the government's persuasion, and were intensified by the financial problems which forced firms like the motor company Kia and the steel company Hanbo, to seek protection from bankruptcy in the courts. The changes are accelerating, but have come relatively late and have not matched the depth of the cuts in diversification which were seen in Europe and America.

Western Firms

Many large Western firms retain a wide range of different activities and, in spite of their refocusing, they are still diversified by any reasonable standards. They retain a range of core activities which require a variety of different skills and/or extend across a number of distinct value chains. From among the many possible examples we will consider three which illustrate certain key features of the balance between diversification and downscoping.

Rio Tinto

First, consider the case of Rio Tinto (formerly RTZ-CRA), which is the world's largest mining company. It is now sharply focused on mining in comparison with some of its competitors such as Anglo-American which have spread into non-mining activities, and also in comparison with its own past history: the original RTZ, which was formed by a merger between the Rio Tinto Company and the Consolidated Zinc Corporation in 1962, was more highly diversified with interests in chemicals and cement as well as mining, but it sold off the peripheral activities in the 1980s to focus on mining. By the mid-1990s, however, its interests included aluminium, iron ore, coal, copper, gold, industrial minerals such as borates, and a range of other commodities linked by the common thread of mining. It then operated in more countries and mined a greater range of commodities than any of its competitors.

Rio Tinto is not a conglomerate, it is a specialised mining company and many aspects of extractive technology will be common to all its activities. Nevertheless, the different commodities have different properties and are sold in different markets, so that the product range requires a variety of different specialisms within the broad specialisation of mining. It therefore involves considerable diversity even though the purists may quibble over any attempt to define Rio Tinto as a diversified company.

BP

As a further example, consider the case of BP, which is one of the world's leading oil companies. BP has undergone substantial reorganisation since 1992. It has reduced its labour force by about 45 per cent, and disposed of interests in food production and minerals in order to focus on oil, gas and chemicals. Clearly the new products represent a tightly focused group: oil and gas share similar extraction and distribution facilities and many of the chemicals are derived from oil. However, the vertically integrated structure of the petrol market has led the producers into new forms of competition (see page 76 above). The retail outlets are no longer specialised filling stations but have become outlets for a variety of products which may include those related to motoring such as car parts, polishes, maps, tapes and CDs, but also extends to include non-motoring products such as groceries, newspapers and flowers. At the same time, as owners of filling stations, the oil companies now compete with the major supermarket chains and not simply with other petrol producers. Hence although BP has become a more focused producer, its vertical integration and the changing nature of competition have forced it to accept more diverse activities within its core activity of petrol distribution.

Volvo

Similar considerations apply in the case of Volvo, the Swedish automotive group. A corporate strategic review was triggered by the collapse of plans to merge with the French car producer, Renault, and in the spring of 1994 this led to a new strategy for the group. The new mission was to focus solely on the automotive and transport equipment industries, and this involved the divestment of those holdings which were not related to these activities. Volvo had previously acquired interests in food, matches and pharmaceuticals in an attempt to offset what it then saw as a vulnerable position as a specialist producer of trucks and buses, but these peripheral activities were now to be sold. Procordia Food and Abba Seafood were sold to Orkla of Norway in 1995; Shares in Swedish Match AB were distributed to Volvo's shareholders and the company was then floated independently with listings on the Stockholm exchange and on the American electronic stock market, NASDAQ; and in mid-1996 Volvo's portfolio holding in the pharmaceutical company Pharmacia and Upjohn was reduced from 14 per cent to 3.9 per cent of the voting rights by means of sales of shares to institutional investors. Volvo's focus then covered a range of automotive products which included cars, trucks, buses, construction equipment, marine and industrial engines and aircraft engines, but also included sales financing for cars and trucks, and Forsakring AB Volvia which provides direct-writing automobile insurance for Volvo and Renault cars in Sweden.

Once again we find that focus on a single value chain (in this case, cars or trucks) may involve diverse activities (in this case, direct financing and insurance), while a clear technological focus does not necessarily imply a clear focus on markets (compare the markets for cars and aero engines) or functions (compare car assembly and insurance). Further, Volvo's reversal of its earlier diversification strategy also emphasises that by narrowing its focus, and thus strengthening its ability to manage effectively, the company may also have accepted a higher degree of risk in the event of a deterioration in any one of its remaining markets. The company appears to have found the trade-off acceptable in this case, but we will return to consider the balance between specialisation and diversity more carefully in the remaining sections of this chapter.

A Question of Balance

These examples – Rio Tinto, BP and Volvo – serve to emphasise that focused firms may still be relatively diversified, with a range of activities that requires diverse management skills. The issue is one of degree rather than kind. For example, a clear focus on a range of technological skills or competencies may translate into a range of products which put a range of marginally different demands on the firm's resource base. The products may have much in common, but each will have its own particular characteristics involving differences in production or marketing or distribution.

These considerations draw attention to the simplicity of our earlier discussion of an optimum level of diversification (page 84 above). That discussion served to show how firms may become over-diversified, but it was not then necessary to include the subtle distinctions which exist in practice between specialisation and diversification. These distinctions mean that diversification is very difficult to measure, and they raise doubts about the value of any simple indices that include nothing more than the number or relative value of the products or services covered by the firm. Any usable measure must allow for the extent to which the different products or services are or are not related, in the sense of using similar technologies or similar marketing skills.

One of the most commonly used systems of classification is that introduced by Rumelt in 1974. He classified firms both by the relative importance of their different products (a single product, a dominant product with other minor products, or a number of products of more or less equal significance) and by the relationship, if any, between the different products. In particular, he distinguished between 'constrained' diversification in which all products draw on a common set of resources, and 'linked' diversification in which the products are connected in a chain relationship so that each product is related to at least one other product but has much less in common with the more distant links in the chain. The former group is therefore characterised by a single core competency whereas each firm in the latter group has a series of competencies which are loosely related to each other. Rumelt then identified nine possible categories of diversification: single business, dominant constrained, dominant vertical, dominant linked, dominant unrelated, related constrained, related linked, unrelated and conglomerate (Rumelt, 1974).

Empirical studies which use this classification have generally found that the poorest performance is experienced by the unrelated diversifiers while the constrained diversifiers maintain the highest levels of performance. These results are instructive, but it would be dangerous to draw the apparently obvious conclusions for strategy without more knowledge of the choices which faced the different firms. The data do clearly suggest that we should question any strategy of unrelated diversification, but in practice the other choices between specialisation on a single business, constrained diversification and linked diversification will in turn be constrained by the pattern of demand in different areas and by the firms' initial endowments of technology, marketing and operating skills. Some endowments may lend themselves readily to a strategy of constrained diversification, but others may not. Any attempt to assess the strategy of an individual firm must therefore consider its initial endowment of resources and opportunities, the resource requirements for each possible area of opportunity, and the ease with which any new requirements can be met. These issues are considered in the following sections.

THE RESOURCES NEEDED FOR DIVERSIFICATION

The rest of this chapter is concerned with the incentives for diversification and the requirements for success. This section reviews the resources needed for diversification, and the last two sections consider the most common reasons for success or failure.

Evaluating Resources

Firms are commonly identified by the products or services they produce, but if we are to understand the constraints and opportunities for diversification it will be better to focus on the resources they can deploy, because ultimately it will be their resources which will determine their ability to take on new activities in competition with other firms which have different resource endowments.

Economists have always emphasised that resource endowments determine production possibilities, and a resource-based analysis has now also become common among business strategists. (See, for example, Collis and Montgomery, 1997. For an earlier essay, see Wernerfelt, 1984, which draws explicitly on the seminal work of Penrose, 1959.) In strategic analysis, however, the economists' broad division of resources into land, labour and capital will be too coarse for the detailed analysis of individual cases. Strategists must refine the list to identify a number of intangible items such as brand names, technological skills, established teams of skilled workers, trade contacts and access to networks, organisational skills and management expertise. These are generally more difficult to define and measure than the economists' concepts, but they will often prove to be more significant in explaining differences in performance.

It should be apparent that the value of a resource will depend on the uses to which it can be put – diamonds are not valuable because they are diamonds but because they are scarce and are wanted for display by people who are prepared to pay high prices. The value of a resource to an individual will also depend upon the ownership of the rights in that resource – as we saw in Chapter 4 (pages 67–8 above) the ownership of residual rights is not always self-evident and a firm will be less ready to develop a resource if the developed value may be appropriated by someone else. It should also be apparent that no firm can do anything without the application of some of its resources. The critical questions for strategy are: which resources provide the most promising basis for exploitation or development? and given that different activities will make different demands on the resources available, how should the initial resource endowments guide the search for new combinations of activities?

The first point to be made is that the strategist's interest is in the stock of resources rather than the flows or current usage. For example, the analysis should focus on the stock of a brand name or goodwill rather than on the flow of advertising expenditure, because the latter simply directs the current application of the stock while simultaneously helping to maintain it for the future. Similarly if a firm can obtain materials at exceptionally favourable prices, the analyst's interest is not in the current price advantage but in the source of that advantage and in its 'life' or security. In practice, the advantage will depend on production facilities, contractual arrangements or bargaining power, and it is these which comprise the stock for future use.

Given this focus, a resource's inherent potential as a basis for strategic positioning may be considered under the broad headings of scarcity and interdependence.

Scarcity

A resource cannot provide a unique advantage to one firm if it is in abundant supply and readily available to all firms, because any initial success in exploiting such a resource could readily be matched by a large number of competitors, and any initial gains would then be eliminated by competition. This might arise most obviously in the case of resources which can be hired or purchased on the open market and are not subject to monopolistic control, but it also occurs if the resources can be reproduced readily by other firms. Even a resource which is currently unique may be of no great value if the potential for reproduction is widely understood and readily available. It follows that a firm which is striving for exceptional performance should seek to exploit resources which are in scarce supply and known to be available to no more than a limited number of actual or potential competitors.

Such scarcity may arise because the resources are unique and non-reproducible, as in the case of heritage sights or some mineral resources. It may also be true for creative artists and media personalities, in spite of the growing tendency for commercial interests to produce and package personalities or groups to meet an identified demand. The scarcity may also reflect particular difficulties in the process of reproduction. It may be that the process is not well understood. As with the breeding of pandas or the cloning of sheep, it may be that the process does not work in a totally predictable manner, and this may be particularly true of the production of certain intangible resources such as goodwill, whereas physical facilities may give a less sustainable competitive edge because they can more easily be bypassed or reverse engineered. Alternatively, the process may take time, so that those firms which generated the resource in the past will have a head start over new entrants. (Compare the experience curve, page 23 above.) The longer the time that is needed to reproduce the resource, and the greater the margin between a developed and a partially developed resource, the greater will be the potential advantage conferred by ownership of the developed resource.

Finally, even if the production process is well known and available in principle to all firms, other firms may still be deterred by the economic risks. In particular, if there are significant economies of scale, potential entrants may be deterred by the dangers of excess supply which would follow from any attempt to build a plant which was large enough to match the costs achieved by established firms.

Any attempt to assess the scarcity value of a resource, however, should allow not only for the availability of duplicate resources, but also for the possibility of substitute resources. These substitutes may often be more difficult to identify, and their assessment will certainly involve more lateral thinking if all relevant possibilities are to be included. The substitution may involve the use of alternative technologies to achieve the same outcome, as when natural materials are displaced by synthetics, or when electromechanical devices are displaced by electronics, but they may also arise from the development of competing end uses, as when strategies based on the control of cinema outlets were progressively undermined by the development of video cassettes (see page 75 above). In all cases, the development of substitutes may be just as effective as the increased availability of duplicate resources in undermining an apparently entrenched position.

Interdependence

The resources which underpin strategies will be more secure if they are tied semi-permanently to the firm and depend upon the firm for their existence. Conversely, the strategic position will be weaker if the resources can be separated from the firm and do not lose value as a result of that separation.

Consider, for example, the case of skilled employees. Such employees may be 'tied' to a firm in many ways – by reciprocal loyalty, by generous pay or by non-transferable pension rights, for example – and an employer will normally seek to secure the long-term retention of key employees in some way. But the employees may still move, and in many cases they are no more than a transitory asset to the individual firm. The sense of permanence may be strengthened if the individuals can be bonded together into a team in which the members draw strength from each other and from other elements in the firm because the team will generally be less mobile than the individual and an individual may lose strength if detached from the team. But even teams are not completely immobile. Academic appointments will sometimes involve the transfer of a complete research team between institutions, and merchant banking provides at least one example of a strategy which included the recruitment of teams from competitors (see page 154 below).

In general, however, individual resources will be less mobile, and less easily duplicated, if they are complementary with other resources in the firm and depend upon those other resources for their value. Conversely, a single resource may be enhanced in value if it can be linked to complementary resources. Groups of complementary resources may then provide a basis for sustainable constrained diversification which gives a clear strategic advantage over other firms whose resources are more diffuse and more easily copied. As an example of the potential benefits, Hamel and Prahalad (1990) cited the range of interconnected competencies in optics, imaging and microprocessor controls which were developed by Canon as a basis for constrained diversification which included cameras, copiers, laser printers and image scanners.

Accumulation and Resource Leverage

The purpose of the resource evaluation is to enable the firm to select, develop and combine those resources which give it particular strengths in comparison with other firms. The successful firm will build a 'resource barrier', which gives it a sustainable lead by enhancing the mobility barriers that may limit the options open to its competitors (see pages 34–5 above). A firm's ability to exploit resource barriers will depend upon its initial endowment of resources, but over time it may be able to strengthen its position by the selective development or acquisition of appropriate resources and by providing an organisational framework in which complementary resources can draw on one another. Further, given that many exploitable resources depend upon the route by which they were developed, and are therefore said to be 'path dependent', the more effective firms will make a conscious effort to retain and develop their experience while ensuring that they discard experience which has lost its value. They may be able to do this more effectively if their employees have a forum in which they can share their experience, are willing to challenge accepted truths and are continually looking outside as well as inside for standards and ideas. Firms may also 'borrow' experience from other firms if they are prepared to learn from partners in value chains or strategic alliances.

Conversely, a given resource endowment may be dissipated by profligate use, just as the inheritance was wasted by dissolute living in the parable of the Prodigal Son. But unlike the Prodigal Son, firms who waste their resources will not find a fatted calf waiting for them when they repent. Once firms have acquired or developed their resources, they should ensure that the resources are conserved, and used with the maximum leverage to yield the maximum strategic advantage (see also Hamel and Prahalad, 1994, ch. 7). This leverage will include:

- *Concentrating resources*

  Resource leverage will be greater if the firm's goals converge to a single mission. This should help to ensure that resources are focused on key steps towards the strategic objective.

- *Conserving resources*

  Resources must not be wasted. For example, they may be used more effectively if brands or technologies can be 'recycled' and used for a variety of related products, while a strategy which concentrates on gaps in the strategic space may be less wasteful of resources than one which seeks a direct confrontation with established strategic groups.

- *Recovering resources*

  Some developments will inevitably take a long time and require an intensive resource commitment before they begin to yield any return. In general, however, resource leverage will be increased if resources can be recovered more quickly. A policy which leads to shorter development times or faster market penetration will therefore also have the effect of increasing resource leverage.

Applying Resources

Any firm may accumulate resources over time and a wise management will develop strategies which speed the accumulation of resources and/or conserve the resources that have already been accumulated. At any one time an established firm will therefore have a bundle of resources which it has acquired through activities related to its existing product and market specialisms. But this resource base may not be exploited fully by its existing product range. It then has an incentive to diversify in order to improve its resource usage.

Two things follow immediately. First, if the diversification is to be of lasting benefit the firm must ensure that the resources it has are those which are critical for success in the new area. If these conditions are not met the firm will have no basis for a sustainable competitive advantage. Secondly, the firm must be able to acquire the additional resources needed to enter the new area. It will inevitably require some additional resources, and it cannot expect to make the transition successfully unless these resources are available on the open market or can be acquired in time for entry.

In some cases the critical new resources may be obtained by acquiring other firms. This is a common choice, but it will be risky unless the firm already has the knowledge which is needed to exploit the acquisition successfully (see Chapter 7 below). In other cases the firm may have to wait before it can acquire the new resources. It may then be sensible to proceed sequentially, perhaps by entering an intermediate market or a related market first in order to acquire the resources it needs for its ultimate objective.

However, a firm may be able to avoid both the risks of acquisition and the patience needed for a gradual approach if it has the foresight to develop resources in anticipation of future needs. This is most obviously true when the diversification is to create new markets. The most successful firms will then be those which foresee future market possibilities, anticipate the resource requirements, and put together the competencies needed, and can do so before others are able to step in and establish an unassailable beachhead. Firms which cannot do this are less likely to be successful, even if they do eventually require the resources they need – managers who lack the foresight and imagination to see new opportunities are unlikely to have the imagination and foresight to exploit them effectively after other firms have demonstrated that they exist.

But diversification is not just about entering new markets. It may also involve entry to established markets. It is then no less essential that the move should be an integral part of the firm's long-term strategy and not just a short-term reaction to unanticipated threats and opportunities. If a firm is to enter an established market successfully it must have a resource base which gives it at least parity with established firms even if it cannot gain a lasting competitive advantage. The new area must therefore be within the core competency of the firm. Diversification will be unwise, almost by definition, if it takes the firm into an area where it lacks the knowledge and capability needed for success.

RESOURCES AND OPPORTUNITIES FOR DIVERSIFICATION

History tells us that firms may easily become over-diversified. A little thought about the basic requirements for diversification tells us that firms will fail if they lack critical resources. Against that background we can now consider the most common motives for diversification, and some of the reasons for individual failures. Many studies define the nature of diversification in terms of perceived linkages between different products, as observed from the perspective of either the market or the technology concerned. But these are essentially *ex post* measures which are used to compare different firms after the diversification has taken place. They say very little about the initial incentives which encouraged the firms to diversify. If we want to look at their motivation it may be more fruitful to do so in terms which reflect the initial process of strategy formulation, and draw on the basic review of a firm's characteristics and context. From that perspective, either the diversification may be encouraged by a review of strengths and opportunities, or the firm may feel that it is forced to act after a review of weaknesses and threats. This section looks at strengths and opportunities. The final section of the chapter looks at diversification which may be undertaken to reduce weaknesses and/or to avoid threats.

If we start with the balance between strengths and opportunities we can argue that diversification may be encouraged by a change in that balance. This change may originate either as an internal change within the firm or as an external change in, say, consumer demand or technical knowledge.

Internal Development of Resources

Resources will develop and change in value over time. As they change, they may lead on to new opportunities, and diversification may then help to realise their full potential.

Development of Services

One form of this diversification can occur when an internal service that was set up initially to support the core activities develops enough strength to compete as a separable activity on the open market. The service department might then be spun off as an independent unit. But it should be retained and developed if it has become, or is essential for, part of the firm's core competency.

At one time or another this has been fairly common for computer services. In the early days of mainframe computers the larger users would often develop their own programmes to complement the basic software supplied by computer manufacturers. Sometimes this would result in high-level expertise which was surplus to their long-term requirements. The firms could not 'sell' their staff, although the staff did exploit market shortages by transferring between employers. But the firms could and did exploit their acquired skills by setting up software companies to sell programming services. By the end of the 1960s the computer service bureau in the United Kingdom included offshoots from nationalised industries like the Post Office and from private firms such as Laing or Wates in civil engineering (Green, 1971; or Sutton, 1980).

Similar developments occurred during the 1990s. For example when Barclays Bank in the United Kingdom decided to outsource its IT requirements the contract was won in open competition by its own computer services department. Encouraged by this success, the department entered the open market to provide IT services for PowerGen, the privatised electricity generating company, and for City institutions such as Dun and Bradstreet (*Management Today*, March 1996). This not only allows the bank to profit more widely from its computing expertise, it also ensures that that expertise is continually honed through open competition and that the bank benefits from any feedback from other operators.

Computing is not the only service which may be developed in this way. Karlof (1989) cites the organic growth of Service Partner from being the catering department of SAS into a supplier of services for other airlines.

Similarly BAA, once the British Airports Authority and privatised in 1987, was once clearly focused on airport operations but now receives more revenue from shops than from airport charges. It has recognised that airport retailing is no longer peripheral to other operations but has become a core competency which may be exploited in partnership with retail concessionaires who are linked to BAA by co-operative concession agreements rather than by conventional leases. In addition to its airport operations in the United Kingdom, BAA has managed retailing at Pittsburgh airport since 1991, and has trebled sales per passenger there despite the shorter waiting times which prevail at American airports in comparison with the United Kingdom. In 1995 it was awarded the contract to manage Indianapolis airport, with the development of retail potential as an important part of its brief. Further, BAA has now extended its core to include the development of shopping malls at locations other than airports. In 1993 it started a joint venture with McArthur Glen to establish a chain of designer outlet villages across Europe, starting in 1995 at Cheshire Oaks in the United Kingdom and Troyes in France.

Development of Marketing Potential

A second form of diversification driven by internal changes in the value of resources occurs when marketing expertise or a strong brand image can be applied to a range of different products. The results are not automatic. Sony has not (yet) extended its brand image effectively from entertainment hardware to computing and IBM failed to establish an effective brand for copiers. Nevertheless there have also been many successes. Examples include Black & Decker's extension from DIY to gardening, exploiting its brand name and its expertise in small electric motors; Toys-R-Us moving from toys to children's clothing, using its brand name to support complementary expertise in purchasing, stock holding and distribution; or Avon Products taking its experience in managing a part-time sales force for direct selling of cosmetics and exploiting it to carry products for other manufacturers in underdeveloped countries which lack an effective retailing structure.

The examples of retailers who take on additional lines might be thought of as a form of product development rather than diversification. This must be true to some degree – after all, at the retail level the selling of baked beans is not very different from the selling of packaged soups or breakfast cereals. Nevertheless there are clear discontinuities which may be taken to define unambiguous cases of diversification, as when the supermarkets in the United Kingdom moved into retail banking. The lead was set by Marks & Spencer, a relatively up-market chain which covers clothing and household goods as well as food, and which extended from store charge cards into consumer loans and investment products. It was followed by the supermarkets in 1996–7. The largest supermarket chain, Tesco, made arrangements to offer credit cards, savings accounts, mortgages and pensions, and car, home and life insurance; Sainsbury, the second largest food retailer, offered payment cards, deposit facilities, loans and mortgages through Sainsbury's Bank; and Safeway initially offered a debit card which could be used at several independent retailers. The supermarkets were seeking to exploit their image of good service and good customer relations at a time when the reputations of many banks and insurance companies were at a low ebb. But they recognised that they lacked some of the commercial skills which are needed for success in retail banking, such as the assessment of credit risk, and they therefore made their moves in co-operation with established operators: Tesco diversified through joint ventures with the Royal Bank of Scotland, Direct Line Insurance, and Scottish Widows for life insurance and pensions; Safeway's debit card is operated through the Abbey National Bank; and the Bank of Scotland holds a 45 per cent interest in Sainsbury's Bank.

This pattern of development in the United Kingdom contrasts with that in America, where stores have generally chosen to offer in-store financial services by leasing space to banks rather than by direct entry. The American experience may have been coloured by the unsuccessful venture into stocks, property and insurance which Sears, Roebuck made in the 1980s, although the moves by supermarkets in the United Kingdom have also been aided by the less regulated and more fluid state of retail banking in the mid-1990s. Nevertheless, the pattern is not universal. Asda, another major supermarket chain in the United kingdom, has chosen to follow the American pattern by leasing space in its stores for branch banks to be run by Lloyds TSB. Asda argued that it was more appropriate for the bank to bear the costs and any risks which might be involved.

Research-Based Diversification

Research strength will normally be essential for entry to a high-tech industry, given that the incentive for diversification comes from some other perceived opportunity. Research may also provide a direct opportunity and incentive to diversify if it produces results which are not directly related to the existing core activities. For example Britain's ICI entered man-made fibres largely because it had a patent sharing agreement with America's du Pont which gave access to a manufacturing licence for nylon, and many chemical firms entered the drug industry on the strength of their expertise in chemical research.

However, diversification which is based on a chance discovery is unlikely to be successful in the long run if the firm lacks the expertise and commitment to continue its focus on the new area. New discoveries do not have to be developed in-house; they may be sold or licensed to other firms, and this may be the more profitable alternative if the other firms have more ready access to the complementary resources needed for their exploitation. For example, when the Calico Printing Association, a specialist in textile finishing, discovered the first practicable polyester fibre for the textile industry they chose to sell the rights for production to ICI (as Terylene) and to du Pont (as Dacron). Similarly the link between the chemical industry and the drug industry has become more tenuous as the nature of the drug industry has changed (see pages 102–4 below), and many of the old organisational links are being broken. ICI separated its biosciences (pharmaceuticals, agrochemicals and seeds) as an independent company, Zeneca, in 1993; Ciba-Geigy sold its general chemical interests to focus on drugs as part of its reorganisation in the merger with Sandoz in 1996 to form Novartis; and the American chemical company Dow sold Marion Merrell to Hoechst, which also announced plans to separate its drug business from its main chemical activities (Lynn, 1996).

In general, while developable assets can offer a sound basis for diversification, the move will be successful only if the firm acquires and commits the necessary complementary resources, and success will persist in the long run only if the new area remains as part of the core competency of the firm.

External Changes and New Opportunities

A firm may acquire and develop resources as it grows, but the use that can be made of those resources, and hence their value, will also be affected by changes in the environment that alter the pattern of demand or the availability of technologies or complementary resources. The effects may be specific to a single firm, as might happen, for example, if a purchaser looks to an existing supplier for a wider range of supplies. But it will generally be easier to observe when it takes the form of major changes which break down the traditional divisions between industries and force all firms to reappraise the balance between their resources and the new pattern of opportunities. These changes may be driven primarily either by technology or by the pattern of demand.

Digital Technology

Consider, for example, the developments in digital technology which blurred the differences between computers, television sets and telephones in the mid-1990s. Before then, television technology had little in common with computing except for the visual display, and the technology for telephone transmission had little in common with that for audio systems. By contrast the digital machines are more alike and use a technology which is as relevant to the telephone companies or to firms like Sony or Matsushita as it is to Silicon Valley. This technological convergence has forced many firms to review their strategic balance. For example, in the early and mid-1990s Sony made a substantial shift from analogue to digital products, and Microsoft increased its interests in multimedia with investments in film production and cable television.

Health Care

As a more detailed example, consider the market for health care. Here, change has been driven by a combination of technical and market forces. The cost of developing new drugs is rising; biochemistry has become increasingly important; and there have been substantial changes in the methods of treatment which, *inter alia*, have reduced the previous emphasis on hospitalisation. At the same time the government agencies and insurance companies who are the paymasters for most health care have become more and more concerned by the increases in cost and have started to press for more cost-effective treatments. This pressure is emphasised by the share of GDP taken by health care which rose from 4.9 per cent to 7.3 per cent in Europe as a whole between 1970 and 1990, and from 7.2 per cent to 12.3 per cent in America over the same period.

Most firms in the industry have developed new strategies in response to these changes. There has been no single, dominant response, because firms have been forced to make adjustments which suit their own particular resource base and position in the industry. Most firms have chosen new strategies which remain within their initial broad areas of specialisation, broadly defined, but there are some pointers to further convergence between the different segments of the health care market.

In Western Europe the initiatives were typically taken by the drug companies. The various strategies have included both diversification between markets and specialised growth with broader coverage of segments within markets. Some firms have sought to achieve greater absolute and relative size in order to reinforce their brand name, gain economies of scale and cover a broader portfolio of drugs. Sometimes this has been achieved by mergers between established giants, as with Glaxo's hostile takeover of Wellcome in 1995 to give the world's largest producer of prescription medicines, or the combination of Switzerland's Sandoz with Ciba-Geigy to form Novartis in 1996. Other firms have sought to achieve size and coverage by a series of mergers with smaller firms, as the Swiss Hoffman-la-Roche acquired the American Genentech in 1990 for its skills in biotechnology, took over Syntex in 1994 to broaden its coverage into painkilling and anti-inflammatory drugs, and bid for Corange in 1997 to strengthen its position in diagnostics. In general, many chemically based drug companies have sought to broaden their base by acquiring interests in biotechnology.

A further strategy has been to combine research-based prescription medicines with self-medication or 'over the counter' (OTC) medicines.

The Anglo-American company SmithKline Beecham was well established in prescription medicines before it became the world's largest supplier of OTC medicines through its acquisition of the American Sterling company in 1994, and Glaxo's acquisition of Wellcome also gave it entry to the OTC market through the existing alliance between Wellcome and Warner-Lambert.

A number of drug companies in both Britain and America have also sought to strengthen their hold on drug distribution. This is sometimes prevented by regulations in Continental Europe, but in America the reaction to changing market pressures has included moves by the drug companies to acquire Pharmacy Benefit Management groups (PBMs), which effectively act as drug wholesalers to minimise drug costs for funding agencies. Medco was acquired by Merck; SmithKline Beecham acquired Diversified Pharmaceutical Services; Eli Lilly acquired PCS Health Management; and Caremark formed an alliance with France's Rhone-Poulenc Rorer and two American drug companies, Pfizer and Bristol-Myers Squibb. The drug companies will not be able to use the PBMs as tied outlets for their drugs without undermining the PBMs' role as wholesalers to the funding agencies, but the acquisitions do give them more options in a changing industry and also provide better information from which they can learn how to match individual patients more effectively with specific therapies.

However, while the drug companies may broaden their coverage of prescription medicines, combine OTC and prescription medicines, and move vertically into drug distribution, they are still focused on drugs that account for no more than about 10 per cent of the total market for health care. A few have gone further than this. For example the British Drug company Zeneca acquired the American firm Salik Health Care, which provides managed care for all aspects of cancer, and not just drug treatment, through a chain of clinics and hospitals. Salik provides a small proportion of Zeneca's total revenues, but such linkages could become more common as the number of disease-specific care providers increases.

Further, although the drug companies have generally led the reorganisation in Western Europe, and Asian drug firms have generally lacked the muscle to have a major impact on the structure of the international health care market, other health care providers are large enough to have had a significant national impact in America and may move out into the international market. Columbia Healthcare, having acquired the hospital chains of HCA and Health Trust, achieved consolidated sales greater than those of the world's largest drug company. It aims to complement hospitals with local networks to manage treatment and provide cost-effective care, taking advantage of the progress in many areas which has reduced the use of treatments based upon hospitalisation alone.

Health care is not a homogeneous market. Previous attempts to combine drugs and medical equipment were not generally successful and it is notable that many drug firms have retained a focus on drugs even as they have broadened their market coverage and extended into diagnostics, biomedical sciences or distribution. But the industry is not in a steady state. The growth of countervailing groups like Columbia Healthcare, and the probable growth of organisations which offer managed care for specific medical conditions, may encourage more firms to see the market in terms of the treatment of disease rather than the manufacture and distribution of drugs. For this to happen, however, the resource base of the companies would need to be developed still further as the markets continue to converge.

Synergy

We have seen that internal developments or external changes in technology and markets may alter the value of a firm's resources and shift the boundaries which previously separated different sets of opportunities. But we have also emphasised that firms need to acquire complementary resources in order to exploit those opportunities, and that they must not only see an opportunity but must also see a comparative advantage over competitors in developing that opportunity. In the conventional wisdom, there must be some synergy between the old activities and the new.

An Elusive Concept

The synergy which determines the extent of the competitive advantage conferred by the firm's core resources, is not easy to assess. A detailed assessment would be costly and time-consuming, and the time required may not be available when the strategy requires a pre-emptive strike or when there is a battle for the acquisition of another firm whose resources seem to be an essential part of the jigsaw. Competitive pressure for a quick response will often produce an ill-considered response. But even if there is no pressure, the assessment will be constrained by bounded rationality and uncertainty, especially when the main features of the environment are changing like sand dunes in a desert and assessments have to be applied to new and as yet untried combinations of resources. The danger then is that, in the absence of any clear evidence to the contrary, managers may be too ready to convince themselves that the resources they already control are precisely those which will give the greatest possible synergy in the new area.

Hamel and Prahalad (1994) seek to minimise the effects of uncertainty by arguing that future leaders of emergent industries will have taken an initiative in the transformation of the industry by redrawing boundaries and changing the rules of engagement. Similarly in Chapter 1 (page 5) we argued that one reaction to uncertainty is to seek control of those factors which may determine the future. With the advantage of hindsight, most industry leaders may be seen to have followed such strategies. Nevertheless it is clear that there are many firms seeking future leadership in digital technology or health care, for example, and they do not all share a common vision of the way in which these industries will develop. The search for dominance does not eliminate uncertainty even if does provide a plausible strategy for trying to come to terms with it.

Further problems may arise if acquisitions or alliances are needed to provide access to the complementary assets for diversification. Networks take time to build and potential partners need to be assessed as carefully as in any human courtship. Similar problems may arise with acquisitions, with the further proviso that the acquired units must be combined effectively with the old. The new combinations of resources which are needed for diversification cannot be effective unless the previously distinct units can be made to work together harmoniously, and it is easy to underestimate the managerial time and effort which may be needed to achieve this.

In the circumstances it is not surprising that many attempts at diversification will end in failure. Some failures will be inevitable, but it is difficult to avoid the impression that many could be avoided by more careful appraisal. We will consider two examples to illustrate the difficulties: AT&T's attempt to enter the computer industry; and attempts by Sony and Matsushita to buy their way into film production.

AT&T and Computing

AT&T, a major American telecommunications company, attempted to enter the computer industry in the mid-1980s. It believed that it could see synergy between computers and the electronic switch gear which it used for telephones, and it expected to be able to exploit its existing contacts with the commercial users of telecommunications in order to smooth its entry to the computer market. In practice, however, although computers and switchgear use similar technology, the markets were very different. Telecommunications managers do not take decisions on computing, and increasingly the computers were to become consumer goods as well as producer goods.

In an attempt to gain a more appropriate balance of resources, AT&T acquired NCR in a hostile takeover in 1991. NCR was then well established as a supplier of computers and business machines, with particular strengths in providing systems for banks and retailers, and although it was probably not well placed for the transition from mini computers to personal computers it seemed to offer AT&T the resources which its experience had shown that it lacked. In practice the hoped-for synergies were elusive or nonexistent. The clash between corporate cultures made it difficult to coordinate the operations of the two units (*The Economist*, 23 March 1996): NCR was hierarchical and resistant to cultural change whereas AT&T was already decentralised; AT&T's staff were unionised, whereas NCR's were not. Further, in practice the technologies proved to be similar but not convergent, and there were few if any synergies in marketing.

In 1995 AT&T was forced to acknowledge the failure of this particular diversification strategy. It reversed its previous takeover of NCR and withdrew from computing.

Sony, Matsushita and Hollywood

Sony and Matsushita are both Japanese companies with broad competencies in entertainment hardware such as television, audio systems and game players. Neither has been particularly successful with their diversification into the entertainment software of films and television programmes.

Sony's interest in the software began in 1987 with the purchase of CBS Records following a profitable partnership in the joint venture CBS/Sony in Japan and Sony's interest in the CBS library of recordings. This was followed by the acquisition of Columbia Pictures in 1989. Sony appeared to believe that it would have a firmer mastery of the hardware if it also had first-hand knowledge of the nature of the consumer demand for software. It may have also have been looking for long-term synergies between audio and video technology and between films and games (Kester, 1991). Similar motives influenced Matsushita's takeover in 1990 of MCA, the parent company of the Universal studios, and both Sony and Matsushita may also have been encouraged by relatively low-cost finance to pursue diversification without a full assessment of all the factors involved.

In practice neither company found particular synergy between consumer electronics and a service industry which is heavily dependent on creativity, and both have been forced to write off substantial parts of their investment. The economics of the film industry has several unique features which fit uneasily with high-tech manufacturing (Vogel, 1994). Sunk costs are high, the profits from a few winners are needed to offset the losses from many mediocrities, and each product has varying, distinct arrangements for finance and production. Costs are inevitably difficult to control when production involves many items in a number of different environments, and although changing technology has reduced the cost of manufacture and distribution, there is little to be gained by using vertical integration to exploit these technical changes because the technology is widely available and success will depend upon creativity as well as upon the effective control of costs. The high sunk costs of a film also mean that returns from ancillary markets are important, and Universal studios probably lost ground when the parent company vetoed a proposed extension into retail outlets to follow the lead set by Disney and by Warner Brothers.

Matsushita withdrew from the film industry in 1995, selling MCA to Seagram. Sony, with a larger commitment in entertainment software, has persisted, and Sony Pictures Entertainment had some profitable successes in

1996/7, but it has still not shown a return to justify Sony's considerable investment.

WEAKNESSES AND THREATS

Some firms may diversify in order to reduce their exposure to risk and/or to improve their growth prospects in the face of static or increasingly competitive markets for their core product(s). However, diversification which is undertaken solely in response to a threat is unlikely to be successful.

The Search for a Solution

Risk and Uncertainty

In principle, risks might be reduced by combining products with fundamentally different characteristics. Any unforeseen environmental changes might then be expected to have different effects on the different products and a diversified firm might therefore be able to achieve more stable earnings over time than one which had concentrated on either of the products in isolation. However, if there is an improvement in stability it is likely to be bought at the expense of a lower average performance because the dissimilar products will offer little or no synergy and may require very different management skills. More plausible arguments support the combination of related activities which have predictably different seasonal or cyclical patterns of sales, although the common argument for combining producer goods with consumer goods which are less subject to the trade cycle may underestimate the range of skills required to sell in two markets with very different trade logic.

Growth Prospects

A firm may also diversify with the general objective of improving the quality of its earnings or revenue if its core product markets are mature or slow growing and/or if it anticipates and fears increased competition. The arguments are tenuous. Markets which appear to be stagnant may still offer good opportunities for growth (see page 29 above); a firm which fears competition in its own markets may not be all that well placed to take on new competitors in less familiar markets; and diversification is not risk-free if it is not firmly based on strength in relevant resources. Financial strength on its own is unlikely to be enough, and it becomes less significant as financial markets generally become more effective at channelling funds towards good opportunities. A firm with substantial reserves might appear to be in a strong position if the reserves enable it to carry initial losses more readily than competitors, but the money will be wasted if the firm is still unable to establish a sustainable position in the new area.

Given that firms are not aware of all the opportunities that face them, it is possible that a perceived threat may act as a trigger to encourage search which will eventually uncover a sound basis for diversification. But, in general, proposals which are driven solely by a search for improved earnings or financial synergy should be treated with extreme caution, especially if the managers lack in-depth knowledge of the new area and/or if the diversification involves hidden subsidies from cash cows which may soon run dry.

Motivation

It is also appropriate to ask who might gain if this sort of diversification were to succeed. Some may argue that employees gain from increased stability, but the bouts of downscoping and downsizing in the 1980s and 1990s do not exactly lend strength to that argument. Alternatively some may argue that shareholders gain from the reduction in risk and uncertainty, but the increased openness of financial markets and the increased range of investment products which have been made available to potential shareholders have made it easier for individual investors to manage risks to suit their own preferences within their own portfolios, without having to accept a particular balance offered by a diversified company. It is difficult to escape the view that in many cases the only gainers will be the managers, but this is hardly a sound basis on which to build a long-term strategy.

Combined Threats and Opportunities

It follows from the above that motives which reflect perceived threats are most likely to lead to effective strategies when they complement and sharpen motives based on strengths and opportunities. Two examples from the United Kingdom – brewing and retail financial services – will serve to illustrate this complementarity.

Brewing

The brewery firms in the United Kingdom have been faced with stagnant sales of their main product. The production of beer has fallen since the 1970s and expenditure on both beer and spirits accounted for a smaller proportion of total consumer spending in 1990 than it had done in 1975. Some firms have responded by amalgamating to gain further economies of scale, especially in distribution. Many have also moved to diversify into other activities such as hotels and restaurants within the broader leisure industry. As a result of such moves one major brewer, Scottish and Newcastle, now derives less than half its revenue from beer, whereas the major part comes from the Chef and Brewer chains of restaurants and from the holiday centres of Pontin and Center Parcs. In this case the threat of declining beer sales has generally been complementary to the motive to exploit new opportunities within the leisure industry as a whole.

Retail Financial Services

A similar blend of threats and opportunities lies behind the common convergence of retail banks, building societies (mutual funds) and life insurance companies in the United Kingdom. There have been several mergers as firms combined to achieve what they believed to be a critical mass, but there have also been a number of moves to diversify as the markets have converged. The true picture has been confused by the moves which several building societies have taken to convert from mutual trusts (whose members combine to obtain mutual benefit from their membership of a trust) into public companies, taking the title of 'bank' as they did so. But several insurance companies such as the Norwich Union and the Prudential have also converted from mutual to public status, and the essential point for diversification is the range of products they offer rather than the change of organisational form which may be needed to achieve this.

Within the market as a whole the life insurance and pensions firms have seen a peak in the total volume of business, and the more conventional firms have also faced increasing competition both from direct selling insurers such as Direct Line or Virgin Direct who do not sell through traditional brokers, and from the banks who have steadily expanded their insurance business. Many insurers have seen new opportunities by holding deposits for customers whose policies have matured, and in 1996 the Prudential Corporation extended beyond this into telephone banking. Similarly many building societies, having first extended into retail banking in response to the banks' encroachments into their traditional mortgage business, have also diversified into insurance. For example, Abbey National acquired the Scottish Mutual company in 1992 and bid for Scottish Amicable in 1996.

Clearly as the traditional divisions between sectors have broken down to allow a single market in consumer financial services, so firms have experienced the twin spurs of both new opportunities and threats to their traditional business. Similar trends may follow in America where divisions set by laws such as the Glass–Steagall Act of 1933 (which separates commercial and investment banking) have been progressively eroded by regulatory fiat, and in Japan where steps have now been taken towards the deregulation of the financial markets.

However, although retail financial services may be converging to a single market, it is still necessary to repeat the strictures against firms moving into areas of business about which they know little. The diversification has not been completely painless. For example, in the United Kingdom, most attempts to combine mortgage lending with property sales through estate agencies did not outlast the stagnant housing market of the early 1990s.

The Search for Opportunities

When the threat is perceived more clearly than the opportunity, diversification is less likely to appear as an effective solution. In some cases there may in fact be very few opportunities, especially if operations are circumscribed by government regulations. This was true, for example, of many nationalised industries in the United Kingdom before privatisation, and has also been true of Japanese financial institutions like the long-term credit banks.

Even when there are no regulatory barriers, however, a firm may still find it difficult to uncover good opportunities for diversification if its core markets and core technology are relatively narrow. An early study of the 100 largest companies in manufacturing industry in the United Kingdom emphasised that diversification came most easily to firms in the chemical industry or in electrical or mechanical engineering, because in these industries the research-based technologies and skills were applicable to a number of different markets (Channon, 1973).

Conversely a firm will find it more difficult to diversify if its core skills are less readily transferable to other areas. For example, this appears to be the case of the French company, Lyonnaise des Eaux, which is the second largest French water distributor (after Compagnie Générale des Eaux) and a world leader in water distribution and water treatment. But water distribution may be seen as a narrow and restrictive focus, and Lyonnaise des Eaux now obtains only 24 per cent of its consolidated revenues from water and water treatment. Its interests include construction (24 per cent), road building (9 per cent), energy and waste management (20 per cent), and special installations like scaffolding and pipe laying (9 per cent), with the balance of its revenue coming from a variety of smaller activities which include the operation of toll roads and car parks, and a small but profitable stake in media and communications. The group claim to find synergy to link these operations through skills in negotiating with local authorities and in running customer account systems, for example, or through research such as that into the use of incinerator residues for road building. But the returns are relatively low and the group has been subject to protracted reorganisation in an attempt to make a coherent operation out of its diverse activities.

In general, the only safe conclusion is that diversification should be based upon clear opportunities which grow out of, and make essential use of a firm's non-transferable resources. The risks will clearly increase if the firm moves away from its natural focus. Diversification should therefore arise as a consequence of a firm's attempts to develop its core resources, and is less likely to succeed if it is set as a strategic objective for its own sake.

6 Innovation and Imitation

INTRODUCTION

This chapter falls into four parts. The first discusses the nature of innovation, and especially the concept of innovation as a process rather than a distinct event. The second section then considers the role of innovation in strategic thinking, and the third looks at an important subdivision of this, focusing on the balance between pioneering and imitative strategies. The final section then discusses competition and complementarity between large and small firms.

THE NATURE OF INNOVATION

Categories: Products, Processes and Services

For society, innovation may be the primary engine of economic growth (see, for example, Schumpeter, 1928). From the perspective of the firm it may involve the introduction of new or modified products or services which are intended to be more attractive to consumers, or of new processes which lower costs or improve quality and so allow increased sales or profits from existing products or services. It may also include organisational changes. The introduction of quality circles or the delayering of a hierarchical structure are examples of organisational changes which may be just as innovatory as (say) the introduction of automation.

In practice, however, although it may be convenient to characterise innovations as affecting products, processes or organisations, these distinctions are little more than mental crutches to simplify our thinking. They may serve to emphasise the most noticeable characteristic of an innovation but this should not blind us to the fact that new product innovations may require new processes. New processes will rarely leave the product unchanged in terms of quality and reliability even if they do not affect the design, and effective organisational changes will improve a firm's ability to deliver quickly and reliably.

Organisational changes which affect the deployment or responsiveness of staff may be particularly important in service industries. But even in manufacturing industry an improvement to the service characteristics of a product may be more important than changes to its physical characteristics in defining the value of an innovation as it is perceived by the purchaser. This will be so especially if the product appears as a 'black box' whose design gives little indication of the quality of its performance, as with many electronic consumer goods, or if the consumer is faced by many competing products of similar design. The consumer may then be strongly influenced by service characteristics such as speed of delivery or customer care, and organisational innovation which encourages this may become an essential component of a firm's marketing strategy.

Innovation and Technical Progress

In many cases innovation will occur as a response to progress in science or technology and reflect an 'invention' or 'technological breakthrough'. This is the aspect of innovation which is generally popularised by the media. But its popularity may be misleading, for two different sorts of reason.

Communicability

First, the invention will be irrelevant until its benefits have been communicated to others. New knowledge will always begin with an individual, but it has no commercial value until the relevant aspects have been transformed into organisational knowledge which can be used by the firm as a whole. It will not be so transformed if the firm is not receptive to new knowledge, and this may well be the case if individuals or groups lack the intelligence or foresight to understand the breakthrough, or if they understand it but see it as a threat to their own power base or modes of behaviour. The knowledge may also remain in an unusable form if the individual is unable to communicate it effectively, either because it is hidden in opaque jargon or because the characteristics which seem clear to the inventor after a long period of careful study are less obvious when seen from the perspective of someone else who is preoccupied with other things.

If the invention is to be accepted more widely, the inventor's tacit knowledge or understanding must be articulated or converted into explicit knowledge which can be communicated and can then be internalised and used to augment the tacit knowledge of other members of the organisation. This articulation by the inventor(s) and internalisation by the other members of the organisation are essential parts of the process of innovation but they may not take place automatically and may have to be managed if the process is to have any chance of success (see, for example, Nonaka, 1991). It is less likely to be automatic if research and innovation are treated as separate and distinct functions than it is if all members of the organisation are involved continuously in the process of innovation.

Complementarity

Secondly, the concept of 'invention' may be misleading when innovation depends on the gradual accretion of knowledge or the acquisition and exploitation of existing technologies in new situations. For example, it is often true that innovations which appear to have a low technological content may still be dependent upon prior improvements in technology. Corporate re-engineering is heavily dependent upon networked systems for information technology; credit cards would be impossible without electronic data processing; and even striped toothpaste requires considerable technological ingenuity.

Even if an innovation does follow directly from a single invention, it will usually require further refinement or improvements in related technologies before it results in a saleable product. Its success will then depend upon the social and economic environment and not just upon its technical specifications, and the innovating firm must combine the technical characteristics of the product with appropriate marketing or other support throughout the value chain. Indeed, it will often be true that the more innovative breakthroughs will require more intensive marketing and more staff training because the benefits of the unfamiliar item may be more difficult to understand.

Risks and Errors

Innovation involves putting resources to new uses which have not been tried before, and so it is inevitable that many attempts will fail. The risks may deter many firms, but those that can afford to do so may seek to cover a variety of projects in the certain knowledge that only a small proportion will come to fruition: the Bible's well-known assertion that 'many are called but few are chosen' might well be used as the motto for research directors. Many ideas will prove to be unworkable, or will produce results which fall short of expectations, but the research and development costs of these failures may be absorbed by large firms and ultimately recovered from the profits generated by the successful projects. Smaller firms, on the other hand, may find that the cost of a single failure is enough to break them.

Most unsuccessful projects will die before they are implemented in production or launched on to the undeserving public, but some will have faults which only become apparent when they are tested by consumers away from the controlled conditions of the laboratory. Even large firms may make significant errors of this sort. One such case involved the Anglo-Dutch firm Unilever, whose interests cover food, detergents and personal products with brand names which include Persil (Omo in Continental Europe), Birds Eye and Walls. In 1994 Unilever launched a new range of washing powders under the brand of Persil Power, but unfortunately the powders had an undetected flaw in the principal catalyst which meant that it would accelerate bleaching and ultimately ruin garments whenever it acted with a certain combination of dyes. Consumers were not slow to identify the flaw and were also prompted by Unilever's main rival in detergents, Procter &

Gamble, who had previously tested similar catalysts and discovered the potential problems. It was fairly easy for Unilever to make technical changes to the washing powder in order to correct this mistake, but it was more difficult to repair the commercial damage. Unilever's market share fell by one and a half percentage points in Europe and three and a half percentage points (to 28 per cent) in the United Kingdom. The debacle also acted as an internal catalyst leading to a substantial reorganisation of the company (Lorenz, 1996; Crainer, 1996), which included management restructuring and the eventual disposal of Unilever's interests in speciality chemicals to ICI.

The Rate of Adoption

It may be difficult to establish the timing of an innovation with any precision. Must an innovation be new in the dictionary sense of 'never before existing' or may it simply be new to the user? The answer will be of interest only to pedants, but the question serves as a reminder that an innovation will not be taken up immediately nor simultaneously by all potential users. In a much quoted survey of the rate at which different innovations were adopted in the American coal, iron and steel, brewing and railroad industries, Mansfield (1968) found that on average it took 7.8 years before half the relevant firms had adopted each innovation, although the time period for different innovations varied from 0.9 years to 15 years. In general the rate of adoption will be more rapid if the innovation offers a substantial improvement over the old system. For example, music lovers may be ready to replace their tape decks with CD players, but slower to replace their CDs with later innovations which offer less noticeable improvements in sound quality; and computer systems managers may be keen to make their first links to the Internet but be unimpressed by later improvements in browser performance which would require them to reconfigure machines and retrain users.

But we must also accept that any assessment of an innovation will be subject to some degree of uncertainty: it will be the potential users' estimates of value that will be important, not those of the supplier. The two estimates may not differ by much if the innovation is technologically simple and represents a minor modification of an older alternative, because the benefits may then be communicated and understood fairly easily. In other cases the two estimates may coincide (*ex ante* if not *ex post*) because the supplier has a proven track record and is recognised by potential users as a guarantor for the innovation. Alternatively the different estimates may converge fairly quickly if potential users can sample the innovation or make low-cost tests of its performance before they have to commit themselves, and this testing is likely to be easier for consumable items which are purchased regularly than it is for more durable items which require a longer commitment.

However, the differences between the estimates of potential value are not caused only by the users' ignorance. They may also reflect errors by the suppliers who fail to understand the logic used by potential customers. The estimates made by potential users will reflect the context in which the innovation will be used – it must match the lifestyles of consumers or fit in with the diversity of products, inputs or processes which have already been adopted by producers. Potential users may take a more jaundiced view if they have recently spent money on a similar item which would now be displaced, or if they expect an even better product in the near future, or if the innovation would cause unwarranted disruption.

Firms which choose to pursue an innovation strategy must recognise the wide variety of factors that influence the acceptance of their innovation. They must understand the trade logic and be able to see how users' responses will differ in different circumstances. They must also recognise that time will be needed before the benefits of the innovations are as obvious to the consumers as they are to themselves. Successful innovation may then offer the firm new opportunities for growth, improvements in profitability, or at the very least, a temporary assurance of competitive survival. But it is no panacea. There can be no automatic guarantee that a planned innovation will not absorb more resources than it returns. Unsuccessful innovation can be the sirens' song which lures unwary businesses on to the rocks.

THE STRATEGIC ROLE OF INNOVATION

Acceleration

The pace of innovation has accelerated. For example:

- Honda's adoption of 'lean production' enabled it to reduce the time taken to develop new models from the 60–70 months which had previously been common in America or the United Kingdom, to just over 40 months, and to change models every 4 years rather than 6–8 years, thus enabling them to introduce new features more frequently (Cusumano, 1994).
- Sony's lead time over competitors for advanced products fell from an average of 3 years in the 1970s to an average of 6 months in the mid-1980s.
- In the early 1980s, Hewlett Packard obtained 60 per cent of its sales revenue from products which were more than 3 years old. By the early 1990s it obtained 60 per cent of its sales revenue from products which were less than 2 years old (West, 1992).
- A survey in the United Kingdom found that the average life span reported by manufacturers had fallen significantly for both products and processes,

while non-manufacturers reported similar but less pronounced changes (CBI/Nat West 1997).

This has accompanied a change in the nature of the innovation process within firms (see, for example, Peters, 1987, or Wind and Mahajan, 1988). The changes are never absolute, but as a first step it will be convenient to describe them in terms of the differences between the 'classical' and 'modernist' approaches. We may then consider what might be gained by seeking to combine the best of both systems.

The Classical Approach

The classical view of innovation in a firm is of an intermittent process which is driven by a central department for research and development (R&D). The process takes place sequentially with each idea developed and proved within the R&D department before it is presented to the operating units as a complete package. Each project may be expected to have a fairly long gestation in order to ensure that the technical issues have been studied exhaustively and that any problems have been resolved to the satisfaction of the R&D personnel before their ideas are exposed to commercial scrutiny.

The R&D personnel are predominantly scientists and engineers, and although their work may be informed by occasional market research or feedback from selected dealers, the nature of their training and the structure of their working environment, in which researchers typically talk to other researchers, means that the products they generate will have a strong scientific content and will emphasise product features which have to be sold to consumers rather than product advantages which are already sought by consumers. The internal politics of the R&D department will give the accolades to those who control the biggest budgets and/or attract the most highly trained staff, and this will give the priority to large projects which involve complex technical problems and promise major advances. By its very nature the process will favour the development of exciting new products rather then the refinement of mature products.

The Modernist Approach

The classical view of innovation may be contrasted with a modernist view in which innovation is encouraged as a continuous process which is everybody's business and not something which can be left to a separate R&D department. It ceases to be an intermittent process involving occasional discontinuities, and becomes part of a firm's continuing response to market pressures for flexibility and variety. This continuous innovation will be driven by a search for small improvements which can be perceived readily by customers. Each improvement may give a clear competitive edge, but any advantage will be short-lived because competitors will also be attempting to introduce continuous improvements of their own. The focus of competition therefore changes like a boxing match in which the search for a single knock-out punch is replaced by a series of short-arm jabs.

Continuous innovation may include the reformulation or redesign of products, rebranding and repackaging, service refinements, simplifications to existing processes or schedules, new methods of distribution or new types of outlet. The solutions to problems or the development of initiatives will be pursued through a number of small projects originating with project champions in decentralised units, and an increasing number of corporations such as Du Pont or Eastman Kodak are now using staff training to foster creativity among clerical staff or professional service staff in an attempt to ensure that initiatives are not left to the R&D department alone (Thackray, 1995). The ideas may then be pursued by teams of people who are involved with existing operations and familiar with client needs, but who may recruit additional specialist support as required. They exist as a team only until the innovation has been adopted or rejected by the firm. The teams must take an eclectic view of the sources of innovation – creativity is essential, but originality is not – and senior managers may set targets for innovation which make it clear that no feature of any product or service is sacrosanct. Speed is essential, and any mistakes must be rectified quite quickly because no single innovation will have a long life. Staff must therefore be encouraged to take risks and it must be clear that occasional failures will be tolerated as an inevitable part of the process.

This modernist approach to continuous innovation may make for greater flexibility and enable a firm to respond to the markets' demands for variety, but it is not without its problems. For one thing the greater pace of innovation may mean that there is less margin for error. It may be possible to recover a single mistake more quickly, but the lack of systematic control may increase the probability of a run of mistakes which could have a cumulative negative effect on profits. The difficulty is probably unavoidable, but the risks may be reduced if local managers are competent and well versed in the overall strategy of the organisation.

Profits may be further eroded if the continuous innovation leads to unacceptable increases in costs. It is true that costs may be reduced by continuous process improvements, but costs may also be increased by the pressure to incorporate more and more obvious benefits into products and by the pressure to produce new innovations on time without due regard for the cost implications. Cusumano (1994) records that Japanese firms have been forced to correct for the lack of standardisation produced by continuous innovation in autonomous groups, by appointing co-ordinating managers to moderate the power of local project champions.

Further, the over-decentralisation will not only miss opportunities for cost reduction, it may also miss opportunities for new product development, because it emphasises improvements within existing markets rather than the search for new markets and new products. Firms which rely solely on continuous decentralised innovation may survive into the future, but may then have nothing to offer when they get there.

A Post-Modernist Approach

Innovation for both Today and Tomorrow

Clearly the modernist approach of continuous innovation has its problems, but a return to the classical model would be no solution, because as we have already seen, that model is inflexible, is ill-suited to the progressive improvement of existing products and is likely to overemphasise technical refinement at the expense of market need. Rather it is appropriate to look for a balance – what we might call a post-modernist view of innovation – which will synthesise the best of the classical and modernist approaches.

Unfortunately a perfect synthesis, in the sense of a single model which will satisfy all objectives, is almost certainly impossible. Innovation for tomorrow needs to transcend existing organisational boundaries, pool expertise from all existing units, look beyond those units for new ideas and new alliances outside the firm, and conceive new structural relationships for the firm. This requires strong central initiatives. By contrast, innovation for today requires local initiatives in decentralised units. Some co-ordination may ultimately be needed to offset the centrifugal forces which act on completely autonomous local units but this should be no more than the minimum needed to avoid unnecessary waste.

The opposing forces of co-ordination and decentralisation may be impossible to achieve within a single structure, and the overall framework for innovation must therefore allow for separate and distinct initiatives to meet short and long-term objectives. The process of continuous innovation, moderated by the minimum level of co-ordination necessary to contain costs and ensure effective group learning from local initiatives, must be complemented by a further process to develop opportunities and competencies in the longer term.

This sector-creating innovation for tomorrow must be based upon fundamental knowledge rather than operating experience. It has a long focus and may take place within something designated as an R&D department, but it differs from the classical model by including science and technology, an appreciation of consumer behaviour and an assessment of strategic space from the outset, and not just the science alone. The objectives may be to change the rules of competition, to redraw the boundaries between strategic groups or to create new industries (Hamel and Prahalad, 1994). Each project must have a clear sense of direction and is likely to combine a number of the firm's core competencies regardless of their location in current operating units. When new competencies are required to complement the existing core and provide the breadth needed for new conceptual approaches, the project team must have the authority to consider and propose new acquisitions and new alliances so that the firm may seek to internalise the competencies of others.

These characteristics mean that the project must be supported at the highest level within the firm, but they also mean that senior management may need to commit substantial resources long before the projected revenues and costs can be drawn together into a meaningful business plan. This is not the work of an introverted R&D department focusing on new opportunities to demonstrate their technical expertise, but of an innovatory team seeking to produce significant changes in the firm's operations. Each projected innovation therefore becomes an integral component of the firm's strategy and must reflect the vision of the senior management.

Process Discontinuities

These two major approaches to innovation – continuous innovation for today and sector-creating innovation for tomorrow – may need to be complemented by a third. In manufacturing industries, distinct arrangements may be needed to cater for significant process innovations if an appropriate strategic balance is to be maintained (West, 1992). The need for this arises because the sector-creating innovations are primarily concerned with new product concepts whereas continuous innovation emphasises the gradual refinement of existing products and processes. Although there has been a general shift towards the development of new products rather than new processes (CBI/Nat West, 1997), it may sometimes be necessary to consider discontinuous changes in the processes used for existing products. Adjustments which involve a significant change in scale or a completely new specification of inputs, for example, may be beyond the scope of continuous innovation. The appropriate approach will inevitably have a high technical content which requires scientific or engineering expertise supported by the experience of the operating units, and there must be a clear programme of work to meet clear objectives. The team commitment has been likened to that of a rugby scrum, or perhaps to power play in ice hockey, where the objective is to make rapid progress through a short burst of highly focused team effort in which individual idiosyncrasies must be suppressed.

This third component of the innovation framework may become more important in an industry as it matures. In newer industries the competitive process may emphasise a number of different product features as competitors experiment with alternative formulations or designs to attract customers. At this stage minor differences in cost may be more than offset by differences in design or performance. As the industry matures, however, and as the characteristics of an acceptable product become more widely recognised and more firmly set, so cost differences will become more important and process innovation will become a more significant part of competitive strategy. Even a highly innovative industry like pharmaceuticals will become more cost conscious as generic drugs provide more significant alternatives to branded products and as more complex methods of synthesis give more scope for savings from improved manufacturing efficiency.

But a word of warning is in order. In the longer term the search for process improvements must be subject to diminishing returns. Increasing research outlays will be required to achieve decreasing improvements in yield as the process becomes more and more refined, and there is a danger that the power play for process improvement may be maintained and even intensified long after the strategic imperative has shifted elsewhere. This may be illustrated by the efforts made by American firms up to the mid-1960s to improve rayon cord for tyre manufacture. The first $60 million of cumulative R&D expenditure improved relative performance by as much as 800 per cent. The next $15 million led to further improvements of only 25 per cent, and the last $25 million of cumulative expenditure was incurred after rayon tyre cord had been effectively displaced by nylon (Foster, 1986, p. 123).

PIONEERS AND IMITATORS

Imitative Strategies

The discussion so far has assumed that innovation is a kind of race in which firms seek to keep ahead of their competitors in order to pre-empt a part of the market. Some time ago, however, Baldwin and Childs (1969) suggested that it may be a race which it is better not to win, and that firms might sometimes be better advised to adopt an imitative or 'fast second' strategy.

An imitative strategy assumes that all the necessary information about a competitor's innovation can be discovered by analysis or reverse engineering so that innovations may be copied quite quickly. It depends upon skills in production and engineering rather than creativity, and the support of a flexible operating system which can be adapted to meet new requirements at short notice. If it is feasible, an imitative strategy might appear to offer some advantages, especially in reducing cost and uncertainty, because the prior innovation has confirmed the viability of the project and gone some way towards establishing customers' acceptance.

On the other hand the opportunities for adopting an imitative strategy have been reduced by the growing importance of networking and by the increased pace of innovation in general. Innovators do not work alone. They depend upon alliances with suppliers and distributors, or even co-operative ventures with erstwhile competitors to achieve their aim. A firm which tries to rely on imitation will have little to offer in such reciprocal deals and will find itself excluded from the networks which help to make innovation possible. Their position will be particularly difficult if innovations occur in a continuing stream so that a full comprehension of one stage is needed to give the skills required for the next. The scope for imitation is then further reduced as the pace of innovation accelerates and cuts away the lead time which the imitator needs to prepare his alternative. For example, Saxenian (1994) observed that in the late 1980s Sun Microsystems believed that it could pre-empt reverse engineering by ensuring that it was able to introduce successive generations of a new product before an imitator had established manufacturing capability for the first generation.

The balance of argument therefore suggests that imitation has become a more dangerous strategy than it was in the 1960s when Baldwin and Childs introduced the concept of the fast second. A firm may still be forced to try to become a fast second if a competitor produces an unexpected innovation or is unexpectedly quick to launch an innovation which several firms have been trying to develop independently. The strategy may also be appropriate in markets which are subject to a slow rate of change and/or in areas which are peripheral to the firm's main line of business, especially if the firm has a good reputation with customers and a sound distribution system which reduce the risk that it will be left far behind by an innovator. In such cases a 'wait and see' strategy may be sensible, so long as the firm is poised to act as a fast second if the need arises. But as a general strategy it is unsafe in any industry where innovation is a significant form of competition.

Gains From Pioneering: The Evidence

Even if all firms were to adopt strategies based upon an objective of innovation rather than imitation, this would still leave open the question of whether it is always necessary to be first at everything. Is it essential to pioneer sector-creating innovations? or is it possible to catch up even when others seem to have a head start?

The PIMS database appears to support the case for pioneering. Using that data, Buzzell and Gale (1987) suggested that on average the pioneers retained a market share of about 30 per cent, compared with 19 per cent for the early followers and 13 per cent for the later entrants. These results must be treated with caution, however, primarily because there is some ambiguity over the identity of the 'pioneers'. In a similar context we might ask whether Christopher Columbus really did discover America, or was he simply a better publicist than Leif Eriksson with better access to world markets than the indigenous population? The PIMS data cover only the surviving firms and so omit any pioneers who failed to stay the course. They also rely primarily on a self-assessment of each firm's pioneering role, and effectively define pioneers as 'one of the first'.

A more precise approach was used by Golder and Tellis (1993) who analysed historical sources to identify the first pioneers for 50 consumer product categories. In their sample the failure rate among the pioneers was as high as 47 per cent on average, and higher for durable goods than for non-durables. The mean current share of the pioneers was only 10 per cent, and the pioneers retained their status as market leader in only 11 per cent of the product categories. In fact a higher average market share and a higher probability of continuing leadership was observed for 'early followers' who entered on average some 13 years after the original pioneers during the early growth phase of the product life cycle.

Conditions for Success

The successful transition from a pioneer or a near pioneer into a lasting market leader depends upon a number of characteristics (see, for example, Chandler, 1990b, or Tellis and Golder, 1996). We may summarise these under the headings of commitment, mass market, user-friendly systems, patience, and awareness of competition.

Commitment

Pioneering demands a strong commitment which is more likely to be sustained by firms who see the new area as a clear part of their core business. Any firms which see the new opportunity as no more than peripheral to their core business may lack the depth of commitment and are less likely to stay the pace. This was observable in the early years of the development of the market for mainframe computers (see, for example, Shaw and Sutton, 1976, pp. 103–4). Firms like IBM, Honeywell and Burroughs retained a central focus on data processing. More diversified companies for whom the electronic data processing was a peripheral interest could not stay the pace, and, for example, General Electric and Raytheon sold their interests to Honeywell, while RCA's interests were sold to the Univac division of Sperry Rand before the latter joined with Burroughs to form Unisys in 1986.

Even when the new business is clearly related to the established core, potential pioneers may still fail through an over-commitment to established products which might be displaced by the innovation. This may be illustrated by the experience of Du Pont (tyre cord) and NCR (business machines) (see, for example, Foster, 1986, pp. 121–9 and 139–41).

The Du Pont example concerns the manufacture of tyre cord for bias ply tyres in the 1960s, before they were displaced by radial ply tyres. Initially nylon was the preferred material for tyre cord but it had technical limitations which could be identified readily by users – for example the tyres were prone to develop flat spots after standing in freezing weather. The key question was whether this could best be overcome by improving the nylon cords or by using polyester as a replacement, and the question was made more difficult by the fact that polyester needed further development so that its ultimate performance characteristics were still unknown. Du Pont was the leading producer of nylon cord and was also a significant producer of polyester. In principle it chose to pursue both routes, but in practice it seemed to assume that it could control the pace of innovation and its organisational structure favoured its existing dominance in nylon. New polyester cords were tested on equipment designed for nylon and run by the nylon manufacturing unit which took a patronising view of the upstarts working with polyester. By the time that the polyester cord met the unit's performance requirements the company had fully committed itself to production capacity for nylon cord. By contrast Celanese, another producer of polymers, had no prior commitment to nylon. It developed polyester cords much more quickly than Du Pont and was able to capture 75 per cent of the tyre cord market in the latter part of the 1960s.

A similar desire to protect established products seemed to dog NCR's potential in computer applications. NCR (National Cash Register) dominated the old market for electromechanical cash registers and accounting machines. It was a fairly early entrant to computing with established contacts among potential business users, especially in banking and retailing, and in the early 1970s it was probably the sixth largest supplier of general-purpose computer systems. Until the 1970s, however, it appeared to believe that computers were appropriate only for general data processing and it sought to protect its established operations by intensive development of electromechanical cash registers. In 1971, DTS introduced the first electronic cash register. Electromechanical registers declined from 90 per cent to 10 per cent of the original equipment market in five years. NCR was forced to write off $140 million of machines and to lay off 20,000 employees.

The general message is clear: successful pioneering requires a sharp focus and must not be distracted by a misplaced desire to protect established products.

Mass Market

Successful pioneers must be able to see how the new product needs to be developed, designed, produced and marketed for the mass market. By contrast, niche marketing of new products may well prove to be a dead-end. The niche may be easier to establish because the special appeal of the new product may be more obvious to a small group of specialist users. But if the product has mass market potential the ultimate gains will go to those who have the foresight to recognise and the ability to develop that potential, and the initial lure of a niche market may prove to be a trap from which it is difficult to escape. For example, Teflon's early success as a surface coating for frying pans which were aimed specifically at the diet-conscious market for low-fat cooking probably hindered its initial growth as a general non-stick coating for the mass market. Similarly the disposable nappy or diaper was pioneered by a unit of Johnson & Johnson (Chux) in 1935, but for 25 years it remained as an expensive luxury for travellers until Procter & Gamble had developed the technology needed for the mass market with their Pampers brand (Tellis and Golder, 1996).

The ability to perceive the mass market was one of the major factors behind IBM's early domination of the market for mainframe computers – by the early 1970s it had supplied approximately 65 per cent of the total value of computers installed in the non-communist world. It was not the first company to enter the industry: although it had been involved with experiments at Harvard in the 1940s, it did not offer a machine for general sale until 1953, and it was then forced to produce an early replacement because its first machine was technically inadequate. Further, IBM's success was not founded upon any particular technological strength (the most significant early innovations were developed by Univac and MIT) and although IBM could build on its existing strength in punched-card calculators and tabulators, the examples of Du Pont and NCR (pages 122–3 above) suggest that this could have been either a springboard or a dead-weight, depending on how IBM reacted to the displacement of its existing skills. What did give IBM a head start over its technically superior competitors was its realisation that the greatest demand for computers would not come from the scientific or defence establishments which had been the early foci for development, but from the more mundane but much more extensive applications in business such as payroll, billing and inventory control. It also realised at an early stage that small commercial users, unlike those in science or defence, would not be able to develop their own software. IBM emphasised the provision of software and service support, and ultimately its reputation for software and its ability to bundle software and hardware together were probably the main elements in its success.

In general, the most effective pioneers are those who envisage the combination of skills and products that are needed to unlock the mass market and are not diverted by the transient lure of niche marketing which may be premature in the early phase of the product life cycle.

User-Friendly Systems

The need to develop user-friendly systems comes as a corollary of the ability to envisage a mass market: it is no good aiming at a mass market if the comparative obscurity of the product means that it only suitable for use by specialists. IBM's recognition of the commercial users' need for relatively simple software provides one clear example. A further example, also from computing, is Apple Computer's initial success in the p.c. market following the launch of the Apple Mac in 1984. Apple pioneered user-friendly systems involving such features as the use of a mouse to supplement the keyboard, and the use of icons on the screen to replace more complex instructions. Its subsequent demise in the 1990s reflected its inability to sustain its lead and extend it to the hardware of other producers, when Microsoft followed and improved on Apple's lead and made its own Windows software more readily available.

Computing may seem to be an extreme case where relatively unsophisticated users need help and encouragement to master a sophisticated product. But the principle is general. All appliances benefit from clear instructions and good service. Products which are difficult to use, have poor instructions or are unreliable are more likely to remain unused, and unused products do not generate word-of-mouth advertising and do not provide the demonstration effect which encourages more hesitant purchasers to commit themselves once they see the benefit of the product in use by the early adopters.

Patience

We have emphasised that successful pioneers must have a whole-hearted commitment to the market. They must not be distracted by temporary setbacks nor by the lure of easier pickings elsewhere. In some cases it may take several years and a considerable investment in development before the product is ready for the mass market, especially if the complexity or other difficulty of production means that the cost is initially too high to allow anything other than luxury or specialist appeal. In such cases the cost of development may prove to be beyond the capacity of a small firm for whom a niche market may be the only alternative, but the ultimate success will still go to those who have the capacity and the tenacity to persevere with their vision of a mass market.

The possibilities may be illustrated by the development of video cassette recorders (VCRs) (see, for example, Tellis and Golder, 1996). The pioneering product which was launched by Ampex in 1956 was aimed at professional users with a price tag of $50,000. The Japanese companies Sony, JVC and Matsushita, working from a base in consumer electronics, could see the mass market potential but reasoned that a price of around $500 would be needed if that potential was to be realised. It took 20 years of intensive research before that target could be attained in the 1970s, but the subsequent gains were substantial. Between 1970 and 1985 JVC's video sales rose from $2 million to about $2 billion, Matsushita's rose from $6 million to $3 billion and Sony's from $17 million to $2 billion. During the same period Ampex only increased its VCR sales from $296 million to $480 million. In principle Ampex might have shared in or even pre-empted some of the growth experienced by its Japanese competitors but it lacked the will to do so. It made no persistent efforts to increase quality or to reduce costs after

1956 and it even sought to reduce its overall dependence on the VCR market. By the time it woke up to the potential mass market in the 1970s it had already been left behind.

Awareness of Competition

If they are to succeed pioneers must be fully committed to and focused on the new markets. If they are to continue in their success they must be prepared to sustain that commitment in the face of future competition. Their commitment must be sustained through the first generation and into subsequent generations of the product.

We have already seen that Apple Computers were unable to sustain their lead once others had copied their user-friendly systems. Other pioneers may be more successful. This has been true, for example, of Netscape Communications which launched Navigator in 1994 as the fastest browser software for navigating the Internet. Microsoft, the world's largest software company, delayed its response but by the end of 1996 it was offering a product, Internet Explorer, with a performance to match that of Navigator. Microsoft supported the Explorer with intense marketing effort, bundling it in with Windows 95 and negotiating favourable treatment from the big Internet access providers such as America Online and CompuServe. Netscape has inevitably lost some ground to Microsoft but it has not lost market leadership. Unfettered by Microsoft's desire to tie its browser to its own operating system, Netscape has been quicker to introduce new features. Its browser runs with a greater variety of systems and, above all, it has retained the loyalty of many business users who have been reluctant to face the costs of retraining staff and of rearranging their systems so long as their Navigator is still satisfactory.

Netscape has been relatively fortunate in so far as the switching costs which discourage established users from changing to new systems have developed fairly quickly. This may not be uncommon, especially for investment goods and/or when adoption involves considerable learning which is specific to a particular brand or style of product. In general, however, the switching costs or other barriers to new entry are unlikely to develop until the industry is fairly mature. Economies of scale may be irrelevant if markets are still relatively small and there is little homogeneity; patents may offer some protection but are unlikely to be dominant while there is still some uncertainty about the optimum product or process; and brand preferences will not yet have set into strong loyalties.

The entry barriers may become more significant as the market matures, but in the early days the pioneers must anticipate the potential threat of late entrants, especially those with established leadership in related markets who may gain from the carry-over of skills or brands. The pioneers should recognise that their best defence against entry is to continue the commitment which first gave them their leadership, and to look upon their status as an opportunity but not as a guarantee of success.

LARGE AND SMALL FIRMS IN INNOVATION

The popular view of innovation is confused. For some it is the absent-minded inventor struggling in a garage to produce a contraption which will change the face of history. For others it is a vast number of faceless men and women in white coats working in super-modern buildings with apparatus which no one else can understand. As with most popular misconceptions, each of these may contain a grain of truth, but neither gives a fair picture. In particular, neither can explain the roles which large and small firms play in innovation nor the way in which small firms' strategies might differ from those of larger competitors.

Strategic Considerations for Small Firms

Strengths and Weaknesses

The general characteristics of small firms may or may not favour innovation (see especially Nooteboom, 1994). Their principle disadvantages stem from their lack of massed resources for indivisible expenditures and their associated lack of marketing power. Their main advantages follow from their flexibility and independence, but these will not automatically produce conditions which are favourable to innovation. Some small firms may gain from the strong motivation which may come when the individual can retain the fruits of success and is not fettered by bureaucracy, but in others the prospect of success may be obscured by the risk of failure. Smaller firms cannot cover as many projects as larger firms, and they are therefore forced to try to pick future winners at an earlier stage. Many will fail to do so. The risk of failure will deter many more who are not prepared to face the risk. But some will succeed, and for these successful small innovators the total cost of a successful project will be less than the average cost of projects in a larger company where the cost of the unsuccessful projects has to be carried by the remainder. The successful small innovators will therefore have the competitive advantage of relatively low development costs.

Other characteristics of small firms may lead to equally ambiguous conclusions. Small firms may develop closer links with their customers but they may lack the marketing skills needed to exploit those links. The simpler management structures will sometimes make them more flexible with better internal communications and less risk of information distortion, but in other cases the informality may encourage eccentricity and leave some smaller firms critically dependent on the continued presence of one or two individuals. Some small firms will have scarce competencies and unique tacit knowledge but others will be technically myopic and suspicious of change.

Like any other firm, a small firm's strategy should aim to exploit the strengths and minimise the weaknesses. The problem is that many of the weaknesses may be congenital. Small scale inevitably involves higher risks and fewer resources, and in many closely controlled small firms the characteristics of the owner become those of the firm so that, for example, entrepreneurship may be inseparable from eccentricity or technical myopia. We should therefore expect that most small firms will make little or no attempt at a sustained innovation strategy. On the other hand, while such a strategy will be characteristic of only a minority of small firms (say, 10–20 per cent), that minority may still make a significant contribution in certain areas.

Industrial Characteristics

This simple analysis of strengths and weaknesses suggests that small firms which intend to adopt an innovation strategy should seek to exploit their flexibility, rapid feedback, close customer contacts and any special skills, but should avoid areas which require large indivisible resources and extensive marketing. They should therefore aim at particular niches in appropriate industries.

Research undertaken by Acs and Audretsch (1987) confirmed that the contribution of small firms to innovation does vary between industries. They used data obtained from the American Small Business Administration to estimate the innovation rate, or the number of innovations made by a firm divided by the number of its employees, and defined small firms as those with fewer than 500 employees. The data were taken for 1982 and used the 4–digit level of industrial classification. Their results indicated that the larger firms typically had the higher innovation rates in industries like tyres, chemicals, industrial machinery and food making equipment – industries which were generally characterised by a small number of large firms with high capital and advertising intensities. On the other hand it was the smaller firms that generally had the higher rates in industries which made intensive use of skilled labour and had a high average level of innovation, especially when the small firms coexisted with a fair number of larger firms. These conditions led to higher innovation rates for the smaller firms in industries such as scales and balances, computing equipment, control instruments and synthetic rubber.

It appears that industries which have a large number of small firms provide the comfortable conditions that allow any one small firm to assume that it has a good chance of survival without having to accept the costs of a risky innovation strategy. By contrast, in industries which have several large firms without being very highly concentrated, the smaller firms will be forced to adopt innovation as a strategy for survival. The clear competitive threat from the larger firms then overrides the risk of failure which might otherwise deter innovation, while the moderate concentration allows the firm some prospect of longer-term success. Further, some of the potentially inferior characteristics of small firms such as technical myopia or eccentricity are less likely to arise or persist in an industrial climate which is generally innovative, and the potentially debilitating dependence on one or two individuals may be easier to overcome when skilled manpower is more generally available.

The Product Life Cycle

The characteristics which favour smaller innovators may be associated with specific phases of the product life cycle. Larger firms with their superior resources will normally be better placed to make the sector-creating innovations which initiate the cycle for a particular product or group of products. During the early growth phase, however, new start-ups may be facilitated by expanding networks of specialist suppliers and service providers, and, at the same time, the absence of any industry norms for design or applications leaves strategic space which can be exploited by small firms, some of whom may grow ahead of the market to become future leaders of the industry. The strategic space will be curtailed as the industry grows towards maturity and price or process competition becomes more important. Small firms may then persist in niches within the total market but will find fewer opportunities for sustained growth and will face greater resistance to change. Continuous innovation may still be essential for continued success throughout the industry, but within their niches the small firms are more likely to follow the pattern set by the industry as a whole and will have no incentive to take more substantial risks.

Venture Capital

Small innovators need more than just a good idea. They also need money, but even more than this they must also have a full appreciation of the commercial realities of business. The importance of this may be seen by comparing the attitudes of venture capitalists in America and the United Kingdom. In the United Kingdom, although there has recently been an increase in early stage investment, it has generally been true that only a small proportion of venture capital investment has gone to start-ups at an early stage of development. The larger proportion has gone to support buy-outs or buy-ins of existing business units (see Chapter 7), or to adolescent companies with a proven track record. Venture capitalists in America have been more ready to support innovative start-ups, primarily because American innovators are more likely to have served their time in business to learn the tools of their trade, even if their ideas do involve unproven products and untried markets (van de Vliet, 1996a). American innovators are also more likely to benefit from existing networks among agglomerated firms, and in contrast to their European counterparts, who may often be forced to consider an international strategy from the outset, they enjoy the potential benefit of a large domestic market.

In 1996 the total venture capital investments in America were approximately five times as great as in the United Kingdom, which in turn were approximately four times as great as in France or Germany. In addition to the commercial differences mentioned in the preceding paragraph there may be specific differences between the national characters: for example, it may be that American investors are prepared to work to a longer time horizon whereas German investors are generally believed to be particularly risk averse. There is however some evidence that American experience may be having a demonstration effect and that the European attitudes may be changing, and becoming more favourable towards innovatory small firms (see, for example, *The Economist*, 25 January 1997 and 28 June 1997).

The ease of exit for investors may be a further critical element in the attractiveness of investment in small innovators. From the investors' point of view, the problem with a financing deal for a small innovator is not only the risk that the firm may fail but also the possibility that it may be very difficult to realise any gains even if the firm does succeed. A successful innovator may be profitable, but as the firm seeks to exploit its invention it will be growing rapidly and will have a voracious appetite for cash. It will have very little cash available for distribution to investors. Further, the investors will not be able to realise the true value of their investment in the firm unless there is a ready market for the shares. Private sales of blocks of shares may be possible but will probably involve a substantial discount and will not provide the freedom which a stock market offers to the shareholders of a large quoted company. The American electronic stock market, NASDAQ, has attracted some overseas companies (in 1996 about 8 per cent of the companies listed on NASDAQ were non-American) but in Europe the markets for stock or shares in small companies are still in their infancy. Britain's Alternative Investment Market, France's Nouveau Marché and, since 1996, EASDAQ (the European Association of Securities Dealers Automated Quotation system), possibly supplemented by the Internet, may encourage innovators by improving the potential liquidity of venture capitalists who invest in innovative start-ups.

Complementarity Between Large and Small Firms

In many ways large and small firms are complementary. The perfect set of characteristics for innovation might well involve a combination of the resource base, global knowledge and marketing strength of the large firms, coupled with the flexibility, originality and motivation of the best of the small firms. These characteristics may be brought together through some form of co-operation – an outright merger would generally destroy the special qualities of the smaller partner – and the business climate has generally been moving in favour of such ventures. We have already seen that many large firms have attempted to make themselves more flexible and customer responsive through re-engineering, and at the same time the changes in the nature of innovation have helped to break down the NIH (not invented here) attitude which once set many large research laboratories against any ideas which they had not originated themselves. There has been a greater acceptance of networking throughout industry, and a readiness to recognise that collaboration may be needed to bring together the range of competencies required for many sophisticated products. In this climate it has become more acceptable for large firms to foster or collaborate with smaller firms in order to supplement their own core competencies. The small firms may have even more to gain from such collaboration and have less reason than in the past to fear domination by, or eventual loss of independence to, their larger partners.

In most cases the collaboration is likely to be limited to that between separate links in the value chain, and most innovative small firms will focus on industrial consumers or other knowledgeable buyers such as universities in order to avoid the prohibitive costs of consumer marketing. In other cases, especially in high-technology industries, the collaboration may be more intense. In the pharmaceutical industry, in particular, large firms may become 'corporate venturers' and it is not uncommon for large drug companies to take a minority stake in small research-oriented biotechnology firms. For example, the drug firm SmithKline Beecham has over 130 collaborative agreements of which more than thirty involve equity investment through its venture capital subsidiary (*Management Today*, January 1996). The agreements allow it to benefit from the diversity of small firms and to cover a broad range of options at what is presumably a lower overhead cost than similar work done in-house. Although some drug firms such as Glaxo do not normally take an equity stake as part of their collaboration, SmithKline Beecham believe that the equity stake helps to cement the arrangement and allows them to gain from any successes made by the small company even though they may not be directly relevant to its own plans.

On other occasions small firms may focus on the early stages of research but collaborate with larger firms for further development and marketing. For example, in the United Kingdom the Peptide Therapeutics Group has stated explicitly that 'We are not in business to complete the clinical development, manufacture or sale of the final product. This will be done through collaborations and alliances with major pharmaceutical companies.' (Annual Report 1995) The group was founded in 1992 around a number of biotechnology patents. It obtained a public listing in 1995, and in

1996 it employed 51 people of whom three quarters were R&D staff. Its initial partnership was with the Japanese pharmaceutical company Mochida, which took a three per cent equity stake and has purchased an exclusive option to negotiate licenses for Japan. It also has a major manufacturing collaboration with Biomira of Canada which initially covers a development programme to optimise the manufacturing process for one of Peptide's drugs. The aim of Peptide Therapeutics is to use collaboration to avoid what they see as the 'distraction and weight' of heavy investment in plant and marketing operations. Provided that they can continue to retain research staff and develop promising products within a reasonable time frame, they see their main strategic risk in their ability to identify good corporate development partners(s).

Some 'foster parents' may be more supportive than others. One which offers very substantial support is the American company, Thermo Electron. Based in Massachusetts, Thermo Electron has built on an original competency in thermodynamics to develop interests in such areas as instruments for environmental monitoring and analysis, paper recycling equipment, biomedical products including heart assist devices and mammography systems, and alternative energy systems. The company's ideas for new start ups come from original research or from acquisition, including especially the acquisition of the Coleman Research Corporation in 1995. Entrepreneurs or product champions are encouraged to develop their ideas within one of the company's existing divisions until they are mature. Once they are believed to be capable of independent survival the units are 'spun out'. The stocks or shares are offered to the public and the unit retains the proceeds. Thermo Electron retains a minority stake in the new company and continues to provide financial and legal services and some R&D on a commission basis, while the new company also gains from its parent's image and reputation for reliability. The arrangement is believed to combine a fair degree of security with the preservation of an entrepreneurial climate as the units grow, and might be likened to the practice of a gardener who moves seedlings from the propagator to the cold frame before planting them out into the full rigours of the garden. The twelve units which Thermo Electron has spun out between 1983 and 1995 have averaged annual returns of more than 32 per cent (see, for example, Hatsopoulos, 1996; or *The Boston Globe*, 19 March 1996).

It is clear that collaboration may take many forms. Some smaller firms will survive alone, accepting the higher risks and greater freedom that come with complete independence. But an increasing number will find that an innovation strategy which includes collaboration provides a more effective way of exploiting the strengths and weaknesses of their position.

7   Divestment, Mergers and Strategic Alliances

INTRODUCTION

The previous chapters have been concerned primarily with the issues that have to be considered whenever strategy is focused in one direction rather than another. By contrast this chapter is more concerned with means than with ends. All strategic decisions about the extent or direction of growth will also raise questions about the method of growth, and this chapter concentrates on two types of question: If strategy requires a narrower focus – a withdrawal from some plants or market areas, increased dependence on outsourcing instead of integrated supplies, or downscoping to focus more intensively on core activities – how might the surplus units be disposed of? If strategy requires additional resources – more of the same resources for specialised growth or new resources and competencies for vertical growth or diversification – how might the additional resources be obtained?

In principle, a disposal may involve closure or sale, and increasingly the sale may include transfer of ownership or control to the existing managers. Conversely a firm may obtain additional resources through internal development or through the acquisition of other firms, or it may secure access to the resources by means of strategic alliances. This chapter gives an oversight of these strategic decisions. It is concerned with the choices rather than their implementation. It is not concerned with the details of (say) the financial or legal aspects of changes in ownership because these involve more specialised technical knowledge.

DIVESTMENT

General Considerations

Chapters 4 and 5 above showed that earlier patterns of diversification and vertical integration have often changed in favour of a greater emphasis on core business. The decision to withdraw from a particular location, line of business or stage in the supply chain is no longer treated automatically as an admission of failure, with the assumption that 'better' management would have been able to avoid the withdrawal. On the contrary, a readiness to withdraw from activities which have no strategic relevance may now be seen as evidence that the management is far-sighted and has recognised the importance of a narrower focus.

Some part of the resulting surge in divestments may be a one-off, reflecting the structural decline of particular activities in particular countries and/or a shake-out of what are now seen as over-diversified positions built up in previous years. But some divestment activity will continue as an inevitable accompaniment of business growth and development. It may occur, for example, if the organic growth of a firm produces business units which cannot be supported without diverting resources from core activities. Unless those units seem promising enough to be accepted as part of a revised core, they must be candidates for divestment. Alternatively a merger between two firms may allow closures to avoid duplication or may require a change in the focus of the combined operation so that some units or activities become surplus to the needs of the new organisation.

Clearly the decision to divest particular units should be taken to meet longer-term strategic objectives and not short-term financial targets. There is always some risk that in the face of a general pressure for rationalisation, a firm may opt for the easy solution of selling off those units which can most readily find a willing buyer. The correct solution is to dispose of those which are peripheral to the firm's core activities even though this may sometimes take a little longer to organise.

Closure as One Solution

In some cases it may be appropriate simply to close the unwanted unit, selling off the physical assets and laying off the labour, or redeploying some of them to other uses, so that the unit ceases to exist. Closure may often be the only alternative when the business as a whole stops trading. But if the business continues to operate, closure will be a fairly extreme route to divestment.

For one thing, the closure of a unit may involve significant social costs, especially if the unit is in a small community which has come to depend on it as a source of income and employment. The social costs will not affect the firm's performance directly, but it may still wish to take them into account. Further, depending on the regulatory environment and/or the strength of trades unions, it may also have to consider the direct costs of redundancy together with any indirect costs from the loss of morale among other employees who may fear that they are next in line for similar treatment; and there may also be some costs for site clearance and reclamation, especially if the site has been used for industrial processes which involved toxic materials.

In general the unavoidable costs of redundancy and site clearance are likely to be more significant in developed economies than in underdeveloped countries which may have less effective regulatory systems. But in all cases the closure will normally appear as the less attractive option if it would otherwise be possible to sell the unit as a going concern.

Complete closure may still be appropriate, however, in either of two cases. First, it may be the only option if the business unit is not viable and operates in an industry in which all firms are suffering from excess capacity. In terms of elementary economic analysis the unit should then continue to operate if the total revenue exceeds the total avoidable costs (variable or direct costs), and should close only if the costs of closure are less than the present value of future losses, defined for this purpose as the excess of direct costs over net receipts. The calculations will be significantly more compli- cated in practice when the closure of one unit involves the reallocation of production to other units with different cost characteristics, but the same basic principles apply.

Two riders might then be added to these elementary rules. The first is that the direct costs must include the opportunity cost of management time diverted from other activities to watch over the ailing unit. This cost may be high if management resources are scarce and opportunities proliferate in other areas of business, and may often be high enough to override any case for continued operation, especially if trade buyers are hard to find. The second rider is that opportunities may be found even in stagnant industries (see page 29 above) and it may sometimes be possible to sell the unit at a price which revises its capitalisation to reflect its earning potential to a buyer who is prepared to sustain the commitment needed to keep it operating. For example, we saw that this may have happened in some cases in petroleum refining in the 1990s (see page 78 above).

The alternative reason why closure may be chosen as the preferred option arises when the unit might pose a competitive threat if it were to be maintained as a going concern by another firm. This threat is unlikely to be significant in the case of peripheral operations which, by definition, are not closely related to the firm's core business. It may be more significant when the firm is seeking to rationalise production or distribution by concentrating its activities at a smaller number of sites and closing one or more surplus units which might otherwise be capable of independent operation. Similarly if a firm acquires a smaller competitor solely to gain a specific resource such as a skilled research team or other special skill, it may choose to close down the unwanted parts of the business in preference to leaving them available to actual or potential competitors. In each of these cases the potential competitive threat to the firm's core business might well outweigh the expected costs of closure.

Alternative Solutions

In other cases where the sale of the unit is not prevented by its inability to perform at a profit nor discouraged by its potential threat in the hands of a competitor, the most profitable route to divestment will be the sale of the unit as a whole. However, the decision to sell rather than close does not end the choices to be made on divestment, because the sale may take any one of several forms. Consider, for example, the recent experience of the United Kingdom chemical company, ICI, which has moved away from its previous involvement in biosciences and from bulk to speciality chemicals. During the 1990s its divestments have included the following:

- In 1997 the bulk of ICI's industrial chemicals business was sold to DuPont of America. Five years previously ICI had sold its fibres business to DuPont and acquired the latter's acrylics business in return. The proceeds of the 1997 sale were used primarily to finance ICI's earlier acquisition of four companies producing speciality chemicals – National Starch (America), Quest and Unichema (the Netherlands) and Crosfields (Britain) – which were purchased from Unilever, the Anglo-Dutch consumer products group which in turn was narrowing its focus on to food, detergents and 'personal products'.
- In 1993 the biosciences unit (pharmaceuticals, agrochemicals and seeds) was demerged from ICI to form Zeneca. Zeneca was established as a public company and in 1996 its market capitalisation was almost double that of the remaining units of ICI.
- In 1991, Brunner Mond, which is Britain's only producer of soda ash for the manufacture of glass and some detergents, was bought from ICI by its management. It remained as a private company until floated on the stock market in 1996. It had previously been an independent company founded in 1874 and was one of the four founding companies which merged to create ICI in 1926.

These examples of ICI's experience identify three alternative routes to divestment: a trade sale of units to another firm; a demerger into two or more separate parts; and a management buyout. We will consider each of these in turn.

Trade Sales

The sale of business units from one firm to another is quite common. In addition to the example of ICI/DuPont/Unilever quoted above, earlier chapters have included several examples: Volvo and Orkla (page 90), Matsushita and Seagram (page 106); and Daimler Benz's disposal of its interests in energy systems and automation equipment (page 2). The technical details of such deals are commonly handled by merchant banks acting as financial intermediaries between buyer and seller. The transactions will be relatively straightforward if the operations are already decentralised so that the subsidiary units can be decoupled readily from the rest of the organisation: by contrast, Zeneca's demerger from ICI involved splitting 520 different subsidiary companies in 180 different countries or territories (Lynn, 1996). On the other hand the arrangements will be more difficult and less satisfactory for the seller if the potential buyers are only interested in selected parts of existing subsidiaries or operating units, and in such cases it may be appropriate to consider alternative means for divestment (see pages 140–1).

In general, prior contact between buyer and seller as business partners, clients or suppliers may help to increase the information available to both parties and so smooth the transfer of ownership. An extreme example of this may occur when two firms share a jointly owned subsidiary. With the passage of time one partner may develop a new or narrower focus which excludes the subsidiary, and may then readily transfer ownership to its partner. An example from the United Kingdom is the Do It All chain of DIY shops which was once jointly owned by Boots The Chemist, primarily a retail chain with extensive interests in over-the-counter medicines, and W.H. Smith, primarily a retail and wholesale distributor of books, newspapers and magazines. Boots had acquired the Payless DIY chain as part of its acquisition of Ward White, and this was merged with Smith's Do It All subsidiary as a joint venture in 1990. The DIY market as a whole suffered badly from the collapse of the United Kingdom housing market in the first half of the 1990s, because a family will usually increase their expenditure on DIY whenever they move house. W.H. Smith lacked the staying power and was seeking a narrower focus, having already divested its business supplies operation. Boots was able to take a longer-term view and to ride out the downturn: it acquired full control in 1996 for a nominal sum of one pound, and W.H. Smith agreed to contribute an additional £50 million over five years to complete the divestment.

However, while Boots retained its interest in the out-of-town DIY superstores, it chose to dispose of its home decoration subsidiary, A.G. Stanley, in 1997. The AGS chain (Fads and Homebase) were primarily High Street retailers with a limited product range and they had not been able to compete profitably with the large superstores. Boots disposed of its shares in AGS, paying Alchemy Partners over £7.5 million to take full responsibility for all property rentals and for the 2,400 staff in AGS. Clearly in some cases a trade sale with a negative price may still be preferable to the choice between closure and retention.

In most cases such as these a trade sale means that one firm's peripheral interests become part of another firm's core. In the past the acquirer might well have been a conglomerate with no more than a financial interest in the purchased units, but the general decline of conglomerates has reduced the population of willing buyers, and at least one attempt to build primarily on the divestments of others has foundered. In the United Kingdom, the Facia group enjoyed temporary success with the purchase of a number of retail chains from firms which had over-diversified in the 1980s and were seeking to become more focused in the 1990s. The chains included a number of familiar High Street brands such as Sock Shop, Freeman Hardy Willis (shoes), Trueform (shoes), Salisbury (handbags), Torq (jewellery), Oakland (men's clothing) and Contessa (women's clothing). The group claimed to find a common focus in 'fashion and accessories' and sought to reduce costs, set tighter targets and improve motivation in all shops (Blackhurst, 1996), but it became overextended and was almost certainly covering too diverse a range in too short a time. The Facia group collapsed in May 1996.

Demerger

The creation of a public company with an immediate stock market quotation has been fairly common for privatisation, when governments offer for sale some or all of the shares in an organisation which was previously held in public ownership. Such action was pursued intensively by the government of the United Kingdom in the 1980s and has since been followed by an increasing number of other countries as part of a wide-ranging trend to reduce the involvement of government in activities which may be operated by the public sector.

An immediate public quotation for divested units of a public company is less common. The units must be large enough to justify a public quotation and must be immediately viable as free-standing units if they are to avoid a hostile takeover by some other company. In practice, even when the break-up is clearly justified in the longer term, there must be some short-term risk that the new companies will be exposed for a time like a crab without a shell as they seek to establish themselves. Conversely the scale of the change needed to obtain immediate public status for a divested unit will have a profound effect upon the parent company and, in any case, will not be relevant for the divestment of minor peripheral activities.

A step change of this order may, however, be inevitable for the separation of two or more substantial activities within a diversified organisation. Such structures may have been formed deliberately as conglomerates at a time when unrelated diversification seemed more appropriate as a business strategy than it does today, and, as we have seen, many conglomerates found survival to be increasingly difficult in the more challenging markets of the 1990s. Alternatively, as with ICI and Zeneca, it may be that two activities were initially related but have become more diverse as technologies and markets have changed over time.

The total value of demergers has increased significantly over the last 10–15 years. In America, as a proportion of the total value of corporate divestitures, demergers or break-ups varied between 1 and 12 per cent during the 1980s but rose to between 8 and 37 per cent in the first half of the 1990s, with a noticeable increase after 1992. In the United Kingdom the increase has generally been less marked: the proportion averages about 10 per cent but varied between 1 and 34 per cent during the period 1989–96. Significant examples in the United Kingdom include ICI/Zeneca (page 136) and the break-up of Hanson (page 87). In America, landmark examples include Sears/Allstate Insurance, AT&T/NCR (page 106), and General Motors/EDS (Sadtler *et al.*, 1997).

Given that conglomerate demergers may be highly desirable, but that demerged public companies may initially face some risk of a hostile take-over, the newly independent company may sometimes be protected by what is known as a 'poison pill'. For example, the newly formed Millennium Chemicals which was formerly part of the Hanson conglomerate (see page 87) and which will operate primarily in America, has a 'poison pill' in its constitution which says that shares will be diluted if anyone buys more than 15 per cent of Millennium's shares without first receiving the approval of the Board. The purpose of such a dilution would be to reduce the likelihood of takeover by enabling all other shareholders to purchase a new share entitling them to significant votes and dividends, and a minimum shareholding in the bidder, in the event of a complete takeover. Such clauses are not used only by demerged companies. Similar steps have been taken by a number of American companies including Dell Computers, Westinghouse and North-west Airlines (*Management Today*, 1996). In America such action requires only a decision by the Board, which is presumed to be acting in the interests of shareholders (Jensen, 1988). In the United Kingdom, by contrast, a 'poison pill' would require the full approval of shareholders, and would be prevented by the City's Takeover Code if such a step were attempted once it was known that a bid had been or was about to be made.

Management Buyouts

Given the restrictions on size and the inevitable risks associated with an immediate public quotation, the most common alternative to the sale of business units from one firm to another is the management buyout, although as we shall see the generic term 'investor buyout' may now be more appropriate.

A management buyout (MBO) occurs when a firm or part of a firm is purchased by an individual manager or management team comprising many or all of the existing managers. The buyouts normally become private companies, although public status may be obtained in due course, and the management team normally secures voting control after the buyout. The MBO was originally associated with distress conditions when a closely controlled firm was heading for liquidation and/or the existing owners were seeking to convert their assets into cash for retirement or other reasons. Subsequently it became more widely accepted as a means of facilitating the restructuring of diversified companies, and the majority of buyouts now come as a result of corporate divestment. In the United Kingdom, for example, after a relatively slow start, the number of buyouts has grown rapidly since the mid-1970s. There were only about 20 buyouts in 1977 and perhaps 200 in 1981, but the number has since increased to between 300 and 350 in 1990 and to over 600 in 1996. Elsewhere in Europe the experience has been patchy. For example, France experienced rapid growth in MBOs after the mid-1980s, while in Germany their use was inhibited by long-term contracts, unfunded pension schemes and a cautious response from banks and trades unions (Webb, 1990, and survey by KPMG Corporate Finance quoted in the *Guardian*, 30 December 1996).

An MBO may often be the preferred route to divestment by the vendor. In turn, the incentive for managers to accept the risks of an MBO may have been fostered by the gradual spread of an enterprise culture, and was certainly promoted as corporate restructuring which removed the alternative of an apparent guarantee of lifetime employment in a secure environment. In contrast to a trade sale where the existing management may be displaced, an MBO helps to preserve continuity and ensure the carry-over of expertise. It may also help to preserve existing networks where these rely heavily on personal contacts. The ability of managers to undertake a buyout depends on their access to appropriate finance, and this has been made easier as venture capitalists have looked for more secure investments as an alternative to high-risk innovative start-ups. The early growth in the 1970s in the United Kingdom was actively promoted by the financial group 3i (then the ICFC division of Investors In Industry).

Many of these points may be illustrated by the MBO which led to the formation of the Compass Group (Webb, 1990). The Group was previously the Contract Services Division of Grand Metropolitan. The Division had been formed in the early 1970s when Grand Metropolitan acquired two catering firms, Bateman and Midland, and combined them with smaller interests in hospital management, club management and security. By 1987 catering was the main focus of the Division and was thought to have excellent prospects in the market for contract catering at the workplace as firms increasingly outsourced their catering provision. However, the parent company was fully committed elsewhere and could not provide the capital needed to convert this relatively small business area into a core activity. The alternative of divestment through an MBO was proposed by the chief executive of the division, but initially Grand Metropolitan sought offers from external buyers before it accepted the principle of an MBO. The buyout of the Compass Group was completed in 1987 with primary support from a syndicate of three venture capitalists. The group sought a public quotation some eighteen months later, partly to raise capital for expansion but also to provide an exit route for the initial investors.

In this particular instance the vendor failed to find an external buyer because potential buyers were only interested in parts and not the full range of the Division, while the vendor did not want to be left with an even more unfocused ragbag of bits and pieces. In other cases potential buyers may be discouraged if they cannot count on the continuity of senior management, as appeared to be the case when Amari, a wholesaler of non-ferrous metals and plastics, was divested from BP in a management buyout in 1981. (Further examples of MBOs may be found in Webb, 1990, or Green and Berry, 1991.)

It appears that some MBOs have yielded very quick profits. For example, the Inspec Group of speciality chemicals was sold to management by BP in 1992 for £42.5 million and floated less than two years later for £136.4 million after profits had more than doubled. Similarly Porterbrook Leasing, the first of three rolling-stock companies to be formed when British Rail was privatised, was bought for £527 million by a management team backed by venture capitalists and sold after seven months for £825 million. Some gains of this nature may be inevitable because an MBO involves the sale of indivisible assets through imperfect markets in circumstances where the value of the asset is heavily dependent on management motivation and it is known that past performance may have been adversely affected by under-capitalisation, as is likely to be true of all the peripheral units in an organisation. For this reason it is increasingly common for the seller to retain a minority stake in the buyout as a portfolio investment.

The downside of the risk involved is that MBOs have also had a fairly high failure rate. Some 14 per cent of the MBOs from major United Kingdom companies bought between 1987 and 1989 ended in receivership, with an average of 10 per cent for those occurring between 1987 and 1994 (Oliver, 1996, using data from the Centre for Management Buyout Research at the University of Nottingham).

The risks faced by MBOs are not caused solely by uncertain valuation. Some operations are bound to suffer as they move from an environment which is rich in knowledge and logistical support to one which is leaner and less protective. There is also no guarantee that the existing management team are necessarily the best group to run the independent firm. Some managers within diversified firms may have been held back because the unit they control is peripheral to the firm's main interests, but in other cases the peripheral status of the units may reflect unimaginative or unadventurous management. The first group may well flourish after an MBO but the second group are even less likely to succeed independently than they did as members of a larger organisation.

Because of the risks associated with some MBOs, an increasing number of venture capitalists took the initiative in promoting the MBI or management buy-in, in which they appointed key members of a new management team for the bought-out unit. Further, in an increasing number of cases the initiatives are now taken by the venture capitalists from the outset, rather than by the managers of the bought-out units, and the investor buyout

(IBO) or financial purchase is replacing the MBO. In an IBO, sometimes called a 'bought deal', the venture capitalist acts as principal, buying the target company outright, retaining the equity, and offering the management team a much smaller stake. One possible variant of this approach was involved in the sale by Boots of its home decoration subsidiary, A.G. Stanley (page 137). In that case, the purchaser, Alchemy Partners, was a venture capital operation set up in January 1997 with the financial support of a number of financial institutions and pension funds.

The development of the IBO in the United Kingdom gives an apparent convergence towards the American system of the leveraged buyout, so-called because of the high leverage or gearing of debt on equity as money is borrowed to purchase the ownership of the assets. The purchased units frequently become public companies and some or all of the assets may subsequently be sold and part of the proceeds used to repay the debt. The system has been used for management buyouts, as in the United Kingdom, but in America it has also been used by specialised buyout firms to acquire larger companies, as with the acquisition of Beatrice in 1986 and RJR Nabisco in 1989 by Kohlberg, Kravis and Roberts (see, for example, Gaughan, 1991). Since the late 1980s, however, the number of leveraged buyouts has declined as investors have taken a more cautious view of the junk bonds which were often used to finance them.

MERGERS AND INTERNAL GROWTH

When firms are growing, whether to expand their existing lines of business or to diversify into new lines, they may have a choice between alternative methods. They may opt for internal growth through the creation of new facilities and the recruitment and training of new personnel, or they may choose to grow externally through merger or acquisition to combine the existing resources of separate firms. This section looks at the choice between these alternatives. In practice, firms may also consider alliances which stop short of full merger and these will be considered in the final section of this chapter.

In some cases the choice between internal and external growth may be more apparent than real. For example, the external route may be the only possibility if scarce resources are not reproducible and are already controlled by other firms. On other occasions external growth may be discouraged by the antitrust authorities or made impossible by the complete absence of suitable merger partners, so that internal growth becomes the only realistic option. In most cases, however, a choice will have to be made, and it may readily be presented as a choice between two evils: why grow internally if you can buy a ready made solution to your problems? why grow externally and acquire somebody else's problems? This section will try to present a balanced overview of the options, emphasising that external growth should be chosen only when it is the right option, and not simply because it seems to be the easy option. The discussion begins with the case for internal rather than external growth.

Internal Growth

The case for internal growth includes the potential disadvantages of external growth. The case may be summarised under six headings: goodness of fit, networking, costs of acquisition, post-merger rationalisation, the relative effects on profits, and the relative effects on innovativeness.

Goodness of Fit

In principle, a firm which grows internally should be able to ensure that any new facilities are designed precisely to match its requirements, whereas a firm which grows externally may find that it has acquired a ragbag of bits and pieces in addition to the resources it was targeting. The risk that this will happen will be greater if the acquisition involves a hostile takeover which is resisted by the management of the acquired firm, because in that case the potential buyer will be denied access to all relevant internal information until after the purchase has been completed.

Further, internal growth will normally allow a continuous incremental progression which gives the maximum opportunity for organisational learning and preserves the culture of the organisation, whereas external growth may be dogged by a clash of cultures between the new partners, as in the case of AT&T/NCR (pages 105–6 above).

Networking

Internal growth may make it easier to preserve established networks which might be upset by a merger, and in turn a well-established network of relationships with other firms may lessen the perceived need for external growth. For example, external growth has generally been used more intensively in the United Kingdom than in the rest of Europe, and this may be due in part to the greater use of minority shareholdings by Continental European firms who wish to influence the long-term policies of suppliers or other partners. In the United Kingdom, on the other hand, the effectiveness of minority shareholdings is probably reduced by the relatively greater strength of institutional investors so that outright owner-ship becomes the only way to obtain an influential holding.

Similarly in Japan, the system of corporate governance has contributed to the less intensive use of mergers and acquisitions (Kester, 1991). Since the 1950s Japanese firms have normally eschewed acquisitions and relied on a network of implicit contracts, reinforced by reciprocal minority shareholdings, to give them some influence over the strategies and/or effectiveness of other companies in which they may have a special interest. Its adherents believe that this system has significant advantages over takeovers because it avoids the spread of hierarchical control with its attendant dangers of bureaucracy and distortion of market incentives. Takeovers have therefore been limited to cases where the survival of an important business relationship is threatened by financial distress or competitive aggression.

Between 1981 and 1987, for example, the aggregate value of American mergers averaged over $120 billion per annum whereas comparable figures for Japan were between $8 billion and $20 billion. Most of the Japanese acquisitions were of small companies facing financial failure and were negotiated privately under the aegis of the firm's principal banker. Even for overseas moves, where the *keiretsu* system might seem to be less relevant, Japanese firms were less inclined to use external growth than were their European or American counterparts, and in 1988, for example, Japanese acquisitions in America were only about one-third of those made by companies from the United Kingdom (Kester, 1991).

Nevertheless, as Kester emphasised, the classic Japanese case against takeovers has been undermined progressively by the increasing volatility of share ownership. Ultimately this reflected the cash-rich position of the major companies and their lessening dependence on the major banks, which had at least two direct effects on the system of share ownership. One is that the banks responded to a more arm's length relationship by increasing the emphasis on the purely financial aspects of their shareholdings. The other is that some of the firms' resources went into portfolio investment (*zaiteku* operations) which do not have the associated operational implications of the reciprocal equity holdings in *keiretsu*. Mergers and acquisitions may therefore come to play a more intrusive role in the Japanese economy if these developments continue to undermine the influence which may be gained through networking.

Merger Costs

A merger is not necessarily a cheaper way of acquiring resources, although it may be so in some cases. For example, it is true that from time to time the total share price of a company may understate the true value of the underlying assets either because the assets are being used ineffectually by a poor management or because imperfect information has distorted the market value. Further, some divestments by larger companies or sales of privately owned companies may be relatively cheap if the vendor is keen to sell and has been unable to develop the assets to their full potential. But in general undervalued assets have become more scarce as capital markets have become better informed and more competitive, and the eventual acquisition price for a takeover will normally be greater, and often substantially greater than the market valuation before the bid was made, especially if the initial bid is rejected by existing shareholders, resisted by existing managers or bid up by a competing buyer. An initial undervaluation is therefore no guarantee that the firm can be acquired at that price. Indeed, especially in a competitive bid, it is quite probable that the assets will become overvalued. During the course of a series of bids and counter-bids it will often be necessary to take decisions under pressure at short notice, and there is a real danger that a desire to win a competitive battle at almost any cost will override the rational appraisal of the costs and benefits of victory. The dangers may be increased if the bidder is 'cash rich', in the sense of having a cash inflow or cash reserves which are greater than those needed to fund immediate projects for internal growth or renewal. The bidders may then be using funds which seem to have a very low opportunity cost and they may therefore be less concerned about the risks of overpaying for the acquisition.

Further, the price of shares will not be the only cost of external growth. Typically the direct costs of the administrative, financial and legal services required will amount to some 3–5 per cent of the total share value, and to this must be added the opportunity cost of the very intensive use of management time and expertise which is involved in planning and execution.

Post-Merger Rationalisation

Internal growth will generally ensure that the new facilities are integrated with the old and any adjustments which are needed to bring them into line can generally be made on a day-to-day basis. Some more significant reorganisation may eventually be needed to meet emergent anomalies, but the timing of this will be under the firm's control. By contrast, external growth poses more immediate questions about rationalisation.

It may be possible to postpone the answers if, for example, the acquisition is one of a series which is planned to build up into a substantial holding. The consolidation may then be left until the series is complete. Alternatively the acquirer may continue to act like a holding company which allocates finance but leaves the operations of the acquired firm largely unaffected, although, as we have seen, the financial case for this form of operation declines as markets become more effective. In most cases, therefore, it will be necessary to integrate the operations of the two organisations more closely, and this can make very heavy demands on management time. As an example, consider the acquisition of the British merchant bankers SG Warburg by the International Finance Division of the Swiss Bank Corporation (SBC) in 1995. The acquisition was made in order to strengthen the division's position as a global investment bank with a clear European home base, and after the acquisition the Division was renamed 'SBC Warburg – a Division of the Swiss Bank Corporation'. Some systems had to be integrated within a matter of days, and this was achieved for an integrated EDP system in London and for the adoption of SBC's system of risk control throughout SBC Warburg. Some other changes could be introduced quite quickly, and the integration of specific business areas was generally easier when one or other partner had previously been predominant as in the case of asset management and foreign exchange business. Other areas took longer to integrate and in some cases, as in the Corporate Finance business area, the merger prompted a fundamental reorganisation of all the accountable units. Wherever possible, operations were rationalised through SBC branches so as to take advantage of SBC's stronger capital base and credit rating, but exceptions were made where the maintenance of SG Warburg branches or subsidiaries was required or convenient for regulatory reasons, as in China, Taiwan and South Korea. SG Warburg's joint ventures in Italy and Canada were preserved but co-operation with a local partner in South Africa was terminated and replaced by a new acquisition. As a result of the changes, SBC Warburg's employment was reduced from 10,750 to 9,461 full-time equivalents by the end of 1995. The changes took six months to complete and at the end of that period the company still had to disengage itself from one major contract and was still awaiting approval by the Federal Reserve Board for the integration of its securities businesses in America. The reorganisation was undertaken at what SBC claimed to be an unprecedented pace, and in general an allowance of only six months to digest a strategic merger of this kind would probably be very optimistic. (For further detail, see SBC Annual Report 1995.)

The Effect on Profits

There have been numerous studies of the effects of mergers and acquisitions on company performance. These generally focus either on the stock market valuations of the companies concerned or on their accounting profits. Neither is perfect. Valuation studies may be critically dependent on the size of the window through which the observations are made – if the window covers a longer period of time the valuations may be less subject to purely speculative moves but may be influenced more strongly by factors which have nothing to do with the merger. Care will also be needed if the changes in market valuation are assumed to indicate the underlying worth of the merger, because the markets have not always behaved consistently to different mergers at different times (see especially Shleifer and Vishny, 1991). On the other hand it is widely accepted that accounting data provide very imperfect measures of profitability. Both types of study also suffer from the difficulty of defining appropriate comparators. Changes in stock market valuation have to be compared with the changes occurring for comparable non-merging companies, but how is 'comparable' to be defined, given that all firms are more or less unique combinations of resources? Similarly accounting studies ought to compare the trend of profits after the merger with what would have happened if the merger had not taken place, but in practice they can only compare profits before and after the merger and, at best, can only make imperfect allowances for what might otherwise have happened.

These imperfections will inevitably introduce a lot of noise into the comparisons, but the same findings have been observed too often for the results to be dismissed simply as imperfections in the data. They are not generally supportive of the case for external growth. If we ignore the many qualifications and refinements which adorn the best of the studies, the basic results may be summarised as follows. (For more detailed summaries, see Sutton, 1980, for studies relating to the 1960s and 1970s; and Black, 1989, for later studies mostly from the mid-1980s; see also Ravenscraft and Scherer, 1987.)

(1) The shareholders of the acquired firms may expect to gain substantially from a takeover or merger. The share valuation of the target firm generally increases by 20–35 per cent more than the market as a whole during the period covered by the 'window'.
(2) The shareholders of the bidding firm do not gain. After the general market changes have been allowed for, the shareholders of the bidding firm have at best a zero, and perhaps a slightly negative gain.
(3) There is little or no evidence that profitability is increased by mergers.

These results hardly support external growth as a strategy for the bidding firms. They do, however, contain an apparent contradiction: if there are no gains in profitability, but substantial capital gains for the shareholders of the sellers, we might expect that the shareholders of the buyers would lose far more than appears to be the case in practice. One possible reconciliation has been offered by Black (1989) as part of what he called the Overpayment Hypothesis. *Inter alia*, this assumes that the stock markets do not penalise the buyers because they believe that any other alternative could be even worse – that is, the markets act as if they believe that the acquisition may at least maintain the firm's profitability whereas any other conceivable action might be expected to reduce it.

Clearly these conclusions relate to the average performance of a number of firms, and the actual results for individual firms will be dispersed around that average. Some external growth strategies will be profitable, perhaps very profitable, but rational expectations should be tempered by the knowledge that this is likely to be the exception rather than the rule. Success will depend upon careful preparation, the avoidance of inflated prices, effective integration and careful selection of partners.

The Effect on Innovation

A further aspect of performance was investigated by Hitt *et al.* (1996), who developed and tested a model which integrated the strategic activities related to external growth with the internal control mechanisms and forms of innovation. They argued that firms which were heavily reliant on external growth would be less innovative because the external growth would absorb resources (including management time) and might also create debt which has the effect of making firms more risk averse. Firms which rely heavily on external growth may also come to rely more heavily on objective financial controls rather than subjective strategic controls, because the financial controls economise on information and facilitate arm's length comparisons of different activities, while strategic controls require a rich exchange of information with extensive personal contact within a common culture. Such a change in controls and incentives may discourage innovation because financial goals encourage short-term performance whereas strategic controls are more likely to promote a longer-term perspective and a focus on strategic actions rather than immediate outcomes.

Hitt *et al.* tested their model by using R&D intensity and new product introductions to measure innovativeness, and primary survey data to provide information on internal control systems. The results suggested that an active acquisition strategy is associated with less intensive internal development of innovation, especially for those firms which are regularly acquiring and divesting businesses. The results do not show that active acquirers cannot innovate. But they do emphasise that a conscious effort may be needed to preserve innovativeness during a period of external growth.

External Growth

These advantages of internal growth and disadvantages of external growth must now be balanced against the potential advantages of external growth.

In some cases external growth may be the only way to obtain key resources which are already controlled by other firms and cannot be reproduced. This may be true, for example, of resources which are location specific such as mineral rights or key commercial sites. But in many cases where external growth is cited as the only option, the claim is made because it is the only way to obtain the resources within a given time horizon. It is therefore necessary to consider the relationship between external growth and the speed of response and, as we shall see, there are occasions when internal growth may simply be too slow as a response to satisfy impatient shareholders and/or to offset competitive pressures.

However, even if external growth can deliver objectives more quickly, the firm must still ensure that the benefits outweigh the costs. This means that, unless the deal can be arranged at an exceptionally low price, a merger or takeover will be profitable only if the buyer can contribute something to ensure that the resources can be exploited more effectively after the transfer than they were before. Further, if the potential gains are to be realised, the buyer must be able to make a contribution which was not available to, or not known about by, other potential bidders, otherwise competition would bid up the price and transfer the potential gains to the shareholders of the acquired firm (Barney, 1988).

In practice, the potential gains may arise from economies of scale, or monopoly, or management efficiency, or synergy, and we will consider each of these in turn. First, however, we will consider the potential advantages of speed in more detail.

Speed

Internal growth is incremental whereas external growth occurs in discrete steps. In principle it is not possible to say that one form of growth is necessarily faster than another over a long period, because the sustainable speed of external growth will depend upon the period of time needed to 'digest' each merger or acquisition and on the extent to which internal growth is attenuated during this period. A long period of 'digestion', during which internal growth is very much slower than normal, before a further external step is feasible, might well allow steady internal growth to yield a faster average growth rate in the long run.

The possibility is illustrated in Figure 7.1, which compares the growth paths of two firms: the steady internal growth of Firm A and the discontinuous external growth of Firm B. At the start of the growth paths a merger by Firm B allows it to jump ahead of Firm A, but a different picture may emerge in the longer run. In this particular case, the three acquisitions by firm B still leave it with a slower overall rate of growth than firm A, and force it to make larger and larger acquisitions each time as it tries to recover the lost ground.

However, the possibility stands as a warning rather than as a necessary constraint. In practice, whatever may happen in the very long run, it will generally be true that external growth offers a route to a specific objective which is potentially faster than internal growth. The route may also be more certain: internal growth carries no guarantee of success, especially when the growth is targeted at unfamiliar areas, whereas the acquisition of a going concern is likely to achieve its immediate goals even if the longer-term effects remain uncertain.

The speed may be especially important when the firm is entering a new area of business, because external growth will then reduce the period of time during which the unestablished entrant is exposed to the risk of a preemptive strike by established firms. It will also be important when the

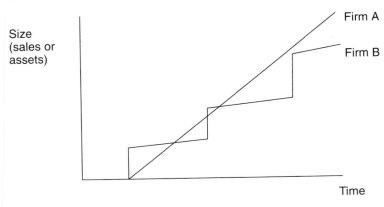

Figure 7.1   *Alternative growth paths*

industry is in a state of flux. New windows of opportunity may exist only for a relatively short period which does not allow time for the more precise response of internal growth. Competitors may then be seeking to combine with the more attractive merger partners, and if their moves are not matched by the firm in question it may find that they have acquired the strength to resist its internal growth and simultaneously removed potential partners for future external growth. Acquisition may then be seen as an unavoidable entry price, rather like the purchase of an option which keeps open the possibility of action at a later date.

For this reason it is not uncommon to find that mergers and acquisitions occur in clusters in particular industries as part of the process of structural change. We have already seen examples of these clusters in health (pages 102–4) and in the United Kingdom market for retail finance and insurance (page 109). Similar clusters in the American defence industry will be considered below (pages 159–61).

Economies of Scale

The resources which are acquired through external growth may be 'more of the same' if economies of scale are believed to be important and the firm lacks the critical mass which has already been achieved, or is about to be achieved by competitors. In such cases, even if the competitors' status is a threat rather than an immediate reality, it may be difficult to grow to the required size without the acceleration offered by mergers and acquisitions. Examples from the international market for reinsurance have already been considered (pages 41–2 above). Similar conditions have encouraged strategies based upon external growth in the retail banking sector, where some services such as credit cards have high fixed costs which require a large customer base and have become more difficult to support as other financial institutions have competed for deposits and driven down the banks' customary margin between borrowing and lending. In America, for example, the number of banks has fallen by about a quarter in ten years as firms used mergers and acquisitions to rationalise branch networks and increase their scale of operation. Examples include the merger of Nations Bank and Boatmen's in 1996 after Nations Bank had grown by a series of nearly fifty acquisitions to a place among the top five American banks.

Size may also be an important factor in external growth when a larger firm acquires smaller firms and is able to extend the benefits of size to some or all of the smaller firms' activities. An example is provided by Castrol's acquisition of Consulta in the 1980s (Hill Samuel, 1989). Castrol is one of the world's largest suppliers of lubricants and then represented about 80 per cent of the total business of Burmah Oil, whereas Consulta was a highly specialised supplier of metal working oils with a geographically small market around its home base in West Germany. Their quality product was combined with Castrol's brand name and marketing strength to give scope for profitable expansion. In general, Castrol's approach to marketing in Europe was to work initially through local distributors in order to minimise overheads until the sales volume justified acquisition of the distributor, which was then used to provide a base for direct marketing into the country concerned.

Competition

External growth may lead to monopoly and/or to the creation of oligopolies in place of polypolistic structures and so may yield monopoly profits if the combinations are successful. There is no doubt that the search for monopoly power was a significant factor in a number of early mergers. In America, for example, a number of basic industries were monopolised during the upsurge of horizontal mergers which peaked during the 1890s, although the later surge in horizontal mergers in the 1920s often converted the near monopolies into oligopolistic structures. For example, both the United States Steel Corporation (USSC) and American Can were monopolistic products of the 1890s, but in the 1920s the acquisition of smaller competitors enabled Bethlehem Steel to provide a more effective challenge to USSC and allowed Continental Can to challenge the earlier dominance of American Can. Subsequently the significance of horizontal mergers declined, partly as a consequence of more intensive antitrust regulations.

A similar trend occurred in the United Kingdom, although the changes started somewhat later than they did in America. The surges of merger activity which took place in the 1920s and 1960s caused significant increases in national concentration, although the effect on monopoly power must be less certain because of the simultaneous increase in international competition in the latter period.

In general, the direct monopolistic effects of mergers have probably declined since the first half of the twentieth century as monopolies and quasi monopolies have been undermined by global competition and, less certainly, by increased regulatory vigilance. This is not to say that horizontal mergers do not occur, but their effects on monopoly power may be less significant than in the past.

Nevertheless the intensity of competition may still influence the motivation for and the outcome of external growth. For example, a firm which is capable of growing more quickly than the aggregate demand for its industry may be reluctant to commit itself to internal growth which might lead to overcapacity, intensified competition and a general decline in profitability. In such circumstances internal growth may require excessive marketing to achieve any increase in market share and may provoke aggressive reactions from competitors who seek to protect their own positions. By contrast, external growth which is effectively undertaken to buy the market share of competitors, may prove to be a more profitable route to expansion. This may be particularly true when the industry's aggregate demand is declining and where there is already actual or imminent excess capacity. In such circumstances internal growth could be particularly destabilising.

Similar arguments may apply for diversification into an industry which is already dominated by one or a few established firms. Entry by merger or acquisition will avoid destabilising increases in capacity and is less likely to provoke immediate retaliation. External growth may therefore facilitate diversification, although it must be emphasised that the diversification must still be justified in its own right, and the new entrant must be able to make a positive contribution to its new partner if the merger costs are to be recovered.

Finally the choice of external growth may be conditioned by competition if it is seen as a defence against the threat of future takeover by a hostile bidder. Several statistical studies have confirmed that the probability of being taken over declines as the firm grows larger, whereas acquired firms are not only slower growing but are also typically less profitable than acquiring firms (see, for example, Singh, 1971 and 1975). The data therefore suggest that a rapid change of scale and a more effective use of current assets may offer some defence against an unwelcome bid. Hill Samuel (1989) considered that some part of the marked increase in cross-border acquisitions in Europe between 1984 and 1987 represented defensive moves against the threat of takeover in advance of the creation of a freer internal market within the European Community in 1992. Once again, however, it is necessary to add a substantial caveat. The defensive moves will not increase profitability unless they are also justified for other reasons, and it is necessary to ask whose interests are being defended by the mergers and acquisitions. The common finding that a takeover normally confers greater benefits on the shareholders of the acquired firm than the acquiring firm, might suggest that defensive mergers are made to protect the interests of managers at the expense of shareholders. Alternatively, if the defensive moves do lead to a more effective use of resources, the shareholders might legitimately ask why the managers needed the threat of takeover to make them identify these strategic opportunities.

Relative Management Efficiency

For some purposes external growth may be considered as an aspect of the managerial labour market in which alternative management teams compete for control of distinct sets of resources (see, for example, Jensen, 1988). In principle a more efficient team should be able to make a more effective use of the resources than a less efficient team, and a merger may be profitable if it effects such a transfer, provided that the team has time to 'digest' the additional resources and provided that the increase in size or diversity does not impose insuperable problems of communication and control. Further, in an industry which is characterised by chronic overcapacity, it may be easier to adjust capacity to demand by mergers which allow the orderly liquidation of marginal assets, than it is by a process of attrition between competing firms which ends in the bankruptcy of complete units. The process of attrition may be protracted if the capacity of the failing units can be purchased at distress prices by others and kept in production with reduced overheads until the end of its technical life, and in all cases the units which fail may include both efficient and inefficient capacity whereas in principle post-merger rationalisation would only select the most inefficient units for closure.

Effective managers will focus not only on the use of the resources they acquire but also on the process of transition. There is always a danger that managers will overemphasise the financial and legal aspects of the transition at the expense of the operating systems, or what we might call the 'merger software'. Drucker (1987) emphasised that successful acquirers should respect the commercial standards of the acquired firm, should plan as if all the seller's managers will leave the firm, and should plan arrangements for the cross-fertilisation of staff between the two organisations. To this might be added the need to think in advance about all the operating systems of the acquired firm in order to develop a clear picture of how these may be interfaced with the acquirer's systems, and the need for a clear plan to preserve and enhance relations with the customers and suppliers of the acquired firm. The more successful companies sometimes prepare for the transition by creating teams of staff who can preserve and focus their collective experience of successful transfers. The alternative outcomes may be illustrated by two acquisitions in the American air transport industry.

The Economist (4 January 1997, p. 60) contrasted Southwest Airline's profitable acquisition of Morris Air in 1993 which followed careful appraisal of Morris's systems and entrepreneurial culture, with the 'autocratic' attitude of US Air which experienced 'years of cultural warfare' after its takeover of Piedmont Aviation in 1987.

Synergy

The final point may be covered more quickly. It is possible that external growth may provide the complementary resources which are essential for diversification. Both partners may lack the full range of competencies needed to exploit the opportunities on their own, and their combination may therefore open up new opportunities which will justify the costs of the merger or acquisition. The possibility is genuine, but the reality may often prove more elusive. We have already seen that it all too easy to overestimate the potential gains from synergy (pages 104–5 above). External growth which is to be justified by claims for synergy must be appraised very carefully, with full allowance for the reorganisation that will be required if the potential synergy is to be realised.

Other Approaches to Resource Acquisition

Finally we may note that the search for complementary resources need not always involve the acquisition of complete businesses. Know-how may be licensed, and physical assets such as plant or land and buildings may be purchased as discrete units. From the buyers' point of view such selective purchases may sometimes be preferred to the acquisition of complete businesses because it avoids the simultaneous purchase of unwanted assets which are bundled in with the sought-after resources, will avoid any payment for goodwill and may also avoid the premium prices which may have to be paid to gain full control of the business. On the other hand such transactions may be less attractive to the sellers if they involve the break-up of units which might otherwise be sold as a going concern and, as we saw in the case of some MBOs, potential sellers may be expected to refuse offers which would leave them with a rump of unwanted resources (see page 140).

The most common exception to this occurs in service industries where critical skills may be embodied in specific individuals and recruitment strategies may complement or replace acquisition strategies. In professional sport, for example, clubs do not seek to acquire other clubs but turn to well-recognised transfer markets in their search for star players. Head-hunting is now common for many management and academic posts, and at least one international bank has used it as a major component of its strategy for growth. Germany's largest bank, the Deutsche Bank, first acquired the British merchant bank, Morgan Grenfell, in 1989. It did little to develop the acquisition until 1994 when it consolidated its investment banking under the heading of Deutsche Morgan Grenfell, and started an aggressive policy of recruitment. It recruited 250 staff in two years from competitors such as Merrill Lynch, SBC Warburg and Morgan Stanley, and then in 1996 it head-hunted the entire Latin American securities analysis team from ING Barings. The recruitments were more selective than would have been possible in an acquisition, and avoided the difficult choice of acquisition target in a market where the most obvious targets were either large and very successful American investment banks or relatively small and tightly controlled British merchant banks such as Rothschild or Schroders. But the selective policy did not necessarily avoid all the problems associated with acquisitions. The head-hunting would almost certainly have led to a general increase in staff costs and did not avoid the difficulty of combining different cultures because teams of high fliers had to be assimilated into a relatively conservative German banking structure.

STRATEGIC ALLIANCES

The Nature of Alliances

Alliances lie between markets and hierarchies. A firm will normally rely on arm's length transactions whenever resources can be obtained readily from a range of alternative suppliers of goods and services that are frequently traded and are not subject to monopoly control. Alternatively a firm may seek to internalise production whenever the construction and use of complex resources are subject to considerable uncertainty, especially if they are rarely traded and are specific to the user. Between these two extremes there is a variety of alternative arrangements. These may vary from simple co-operation between partners in a trading network, through licensing agreements which deal with clearly defined and distinct activities, to the more complex arrangements involved in a strategic alliance.

Three features distinguish strategic alliances. First, in contrast to contracts between buyers and sellers in which one party retains the primary responsibility for decisions, the parties in a strategic alliance will share responsibility. They share decisions, risks and rewards in ways that should be clearly defined when the alliance is first formed. Secondly, in contrast to a merger or acquisition, the partners in an alliance maintain their individual identities and will have separate activities which remain outside the agreement. Thirdly, so long as the alliance continues to exist, there will be a continuing transfer of resources and a continuing dialogue between the partners.

Given these basic characteristics a strategic alliance may take any one of a variety of forms. It may involve any number of firms and the activities may or may not be controlled through the formal framework of a separate, jointly owned company. Some may be highly focused, as in the alliances which were used by many Japanese firms to obtain initial access to distribution and service networks in America in the 1970s and 1980s. Others may be more complex, as in the alliance in the motor industry between Britain's Rover and Japan's Honda (before Rover was taken over by BMW) which included development, research, component supplies and final assembly. Among the international alliances formed during 1975–86 which were included in the INSEAD database (Morris and Hergert, 1987) the majority of cases involved two firms who might otherwise appear as competitors, who co-operated on new product development, often followed by joint production and/or marketing. However, some 15 per cent were vertical alliances with suppliers or distributors, and nearly one-fifth were alliances between three or more firms.

Potential Problems

Strategic alliances are sometimes presented as if they were never more than a second-best solution. Morris and Hergert suggested that 'any other viable alternative would be seized' (1987, p. 15), and Collis and Montgomery suggested that 'many alliances are exceedingly fragile management structures that crumble under the weight of balancing competing objectives and needs' (1997, p. 96). The potential problems include:

(1) In the long run a strategic alliance may strengthen one partner at the expense of the others. This has often been true of alliances which have been used by one party to establish an initial foothold for distribution and service facilities across national boundaries. The alliance may be brought to an end as soon as the importers feel strong enough to establish their own facilities, and the local partners find that they have helped to strengthen their own competitors and, at best, they may then simply be taken over by their previous partners.

(2) Conversely, weak partners may debilitate others: as in a convoy, the pace of the slowest becomes the pace of the group. Many Western pharmaceutical companies have tried to enter the Japanese market through joint ventures, but many have found that their growth is stunted by the limited resources of their smaller local partners.

(3) An alliance will continue to be in the interests of all parties only so long as they share a common view of strategy. In practice it may become more and more difficult for them to agree on common objectives as the environment becomes more and more turbulent.

(4) The division of control within an alliance may delay decision-taking. Many of the problems of information and control which are found in hierarchical structures (see pages 43–4 above) will be magnified in

alliances, especially if any major decisions have to be endorsed by all parties to the agreement.

(5) Information leakage may be difficult to control. Joint operations may lead to the loss of trade secrets which were intended to remain outwith the alliance. Conversely any steps which are taken to cut down the risk of information loss may have the counterproductive effect of making it more difficult to internalise any experiential learning from the project.

(6) Alliances are generally thought to less effective than mergers when 'tough' decisions are needed, as with (say) decisions to reduce excess capacity, which may fall unevenly on the different partners.

Potential Benefits

Nevertheless, in spite of these perceived disadvantages, it appears that co-operative ways of doing business grew rapidly in the 1980s and 1990s. For example, estimates by Booz, Allen & Hamilton suggested that in America the number of formal alliances increased from about 750 in the 1970s to about 20,000 in 1987–92 (quoted in *The Economist*, 2 September 1995). The general conditions that have encouraged this increase are the same as those that have influenced all business behaviour during this period, and include especially the decline of trade barriers, increased globalisation and the accelerating pace of technical change. These conditions have increased the advantages of alliances as they are perceived by firms. The most significant of the advantages are:

(1) One effect of increased uncertainty is to encourage firms to seek control of their environments so as to reduce or eliminate unexpected threats: that is, they seek a 'negotiated environment'. Perfect control will be as elusive as the Holy Grail but strategic alliances may strengthen the firm's hand and give it a broader base of information from which it can anticipate or respond to events.

(2) A firm may gain access to strategically important resources provided that it has some complementary resource to offer in return. This may be particularly important when new products or processes require the combination of a number of building blocks which are spread among several firms in different industries.

(3) An alliance or series of alliances may combine the selective action of internal growth with the speed of external growth. An alliance may bring together the complementary parts of different organisations while allowing the rest of each organisation to continue in its own idiosyncratic way. An alliance will also avoid any premium prices for goodwill which might have to be paid in a takeover, and it may be reversed more easily.

(4) Alliances with a series of local distributors may allow new products to be launched on a global scale much more quickly than would be possible if distribution systems had to be set up or acquired simultaneously in a number of different countries, and yet the alliances may allow more effective control than would be possible through arm's length marketing.

(5) Developments which involve heavy construction costs or other large indivisible inputs may be beyond the scope of an individual firm. Even if a single firm is able to cover the costs on its own, it may still prefer to reduce the risks involved by sharing the cost with one or more partners.

Trends and Cases

General

Surveys of alliances generally confirm the significance of these factors. The INSEAD database identified five major sectors where alliances were common. These were aerospace, telecommunications, other electrical, computers, and motor vehicles. These are all industries where economies of scale are significant, with high entry costs, global markets and rapid technical change (Morris and Hergert, 1987). A slightly later study indicated a similar range of industries with additions which confirmed that exceptional capital costs were not always a necessary incentive. The industries which appeared most frequently in this second list were defence, aerospace and aviation, telecommunications, oil chemicals and plastics, financial services, and food, drink and tobacco (Faulkner, 1992).

In some cases alliances may also be encouraged or forced by legal constraints or business customs in particular countries. In retailing, for example, the growth of some Asian 'tigers' has attracted firms from more mature economies where growth is slower and margins have been curtailed by more intense competition, but effective entry will often require an alliance with a local retailer. In Indonesia, for example, direct overseas investment in retailing is prohibited, and in China local connections are essential for effective operation even though there is now no formal restriction on foreign ownership. By contrast, in Europe, retailers like Marks and Spencer face no comparable restrictions on direct entry across national boundaries although a detailed appreciation of national differences in consumer tastes is still essential for success.

Air Passenger Transport

In other cases, even in mature economies, an alliance may be almost the only route to international growth because local firms are still protected from the full effects of international competition. For example, many flag-carrying airlines are protected by direct subsidies or discriminatory operating con-

ditions. National governments often prohibit foreign companies from owning more than a minority stake in their airlines, and in many countries,
despite the growing popularity of privatisation, airlines are still state
controlled. The allocation of landing slots at airports may also be used
effectively to restrict competition and governments may, for example,
prevent international carriers who put down passengers at their airports
from picking up other passengers for a journey to the final destination.
Some of these restrictions have been eroded. For example, from Spring 1997
nationally based airlines within the European Union, Norway and Iceland
have been able to offer internal services within other member countries,
although this has not affected their more limited rights to fly to non-member
countries such as the United States of America. There have also been some
bilateral agreements between national governments such as the partial 'open
skies' agreement between America and Holland in 1992. But these erosions
are little more than the drip of water on to a rock, and in the face of
continuing restrictions an alliance may be the only means by which foreign
airlines can obtain access to other countries for the effective operation of
trunk routes and for links with feeder services.

The alliances will normally include code sharing (the use of a single ticket
and flight number for journeys involving more than one airline) and the
mutual recognition of promotions such as 'frequent flyer' bonuses or air
miles; they may also include the pooling of ground crews, check-in services
or outsourced services like catering. Examples include KLM and Northwest;
Virgin Atlantic and Delta; the proposed alliance between BA and American
Airlines; and the Star Alliance of SAS, Air Canada, Lufthansa, Thai, Varig
and United Airlines. However these are only some of the better-known
examples. The number of intercontinental alliances in the mid-1990s ran
into three figures, with a host of further agreements for such simpler matters
as the timetabling of feeder services. There can be little doubt that a number
of these alliances would be replaced by mergers or acquisitions if it were not
for the restrictions which protect flag-carrying airlines, although experience
in other industries and the complementarity observed between operators
such as BA and Manx Airlines (page 60), suggest that some alliances will
persist as the industry gradually becomes more truly competitive.

Defence

Chauvinism has also encouraged strategic alliances in the European defence
industry, in marked contrast to the experience in America. Rationalisation
was prompted primarily by the end of the Cold War, which was followed by
marked falls in defence expenditure, and especially in expenditure on
equipment because the upgrading or replacement of durable equipment
could be postponed and so expenditure on these items generally fell more
rapidly than manpower or purchases of consumables. The defence industry

is typically one where large size confers significant operating advantages because the high set-up costs may then be spread over a larger number of units and a large firm can more readily bear the expenditure on R&D and the cost of bidding for defence contracts. The decline in demand therefore increased the pressure for restructuring.

In America the rationalisation proceeded by a series of mergers and acquisitions in the 1990s with the encouragement and financial assistance of the federal government. Some non-specialist firms have moved out of the industry. In 1993, Ford's aerospace interests and the defence computing arm of IBM were taken over by Loral, before the latter's interests were acquired by Lockheed Martin in 1996. Raytheon bought Hughes Electronics from General Motors in 1995, took over Chrysler's defence interests in 1996 and acquired the defence interests of Texas Instruments in 1997. By contrast, Boeing, whose defence interests were originally a relatively small component of its total business, chose to increase its commitment rather than withdraw. It took over Rockwell's defence and space interests in 1996 and acquired the ailing McDonnell Douglas in 1997 to build its defence interests into approximately 40 per cent of its revenues and to make it the second largest defence company in the world. The largest, Lockheed Martin, has also grown by a series of mergers, including especially the merger between Lockheed and Martin Marietta in 1994 and the subsequent bid for Northrop Grumman in 1997, after Northrop had acquired Grumman in a hostile takeover battle with Martin Marietta in 1994 and taken the defence electronics interests of Westinghouse Electric in 1996.

The Lockheed–Northrop deal was challenged by the Justice Department in 1998, but even so the American defence industry was then dominated by just three groups: Lockheed Martin, Boeing and Raytheon. By contrast the European industry was still fragmented and the largest European defence contractor, British Aerospace, had defence revenues which were little more than half of those of the smallest of the American triumvirate. Article 223 of the Treaty of Rome allows European governments to shelter defence contractors from the normal rules on competition and open procurement, and governments generally retain a narrowly defined view of national interest. For example, in 1996 the German defence ministry ruled that STN Atlas must stay under German control. Atlas, a one-time subsidiary of the insolvent Bremer Vulcan conglomerate, produced the fire control systems for Germany's Leopard tank. Similarly in 1997 the French government ruled that it would be against the interests of national security if a foreign company were to buy a substantial interest in the defence electronic group, Thomson-CSF.

There have been numerous European plans for rationalisation, but while the American industry has consolidated rapidly, the European firms have been forced to rely on strategic alliances, which include joint projects for specific items such as the Eurofighter 2000 project between Britain, Germany, Italy and Spain, or jointly owned subsidiaries such as Eurocopter (a joint venture for helicopters between Aérospatiale of France and Daimler-Benz Aerospace of Germany), or Matra Marconi Space between France's Lagardère and Britain's GEC. Typically the joint projects are bedevilled by formal rules which use political rather than economic criteria for allocating work between the partners and which may therefore discourage rationalisation and protect inefficient production units. In the long run, competitive pressures may be expected to lead to pan-European mergers rather than strategic alliances.

Alternatively the European defence industry may follow the path set by Airbus Industrie, which has progressed from a fairly loose alliance towards a more cohesive structure. The group was established in the early 1970s as a co-operative venture for large passenger aircraft between Germany's Daimler-Benz Aerospace, France's Aérospatiale, British Aerospace and CASA of Spain. Its original structure was politically driven. It was set up under French law as a *Groujement d'Interêt Economique* in which all profits accrue directly to members, and initially all work was contracted to members in proportion to their shareholding. The structure has developed over time, however, and by 1999 the consortium will form a separate, jointly owned company.

Conclusion

Airbus Industrie has been relatively successful and has gained approximately one-third of the world market for passenger aircraft. In other cases such as defence, however, it is less clear that competition will allow time for the political compromises to develop into commercially viable solutions. In the meantime, the belief that many alliances among defence companies or airlines are imperfect compromises will dog all alliances, and may undermine the legitimate case for many other strategic alliances which were considered earlier in this section.

8   Summary and Conclusions

Strategy is a judgmental area where there are no nostrums. Any attempt to provide a summary in the form of a brief guide or handbook would be bound to be incomplete and would almost certainly be misleading. It is simply not possible to plot the path which will lead safely to the perfect strategy, and although formal techniques such as budgeting or financial appraisal may provide background information and may have a role to play in strategy implementation, the strategic choices remain as a matter of judgement and cannot be framed in deterministic models.

This should not surprise us. The markets do not reward mediocrity, they reward excellence, and no firm can excel if it uses only the same answers as are available to every other firm. If it is to be excellent, a firm must discover better answers than other firms, or it must discover good answers before the other firms find them. General texts on strategy may help to structure problems but they can do no more: they offer guidelines, not solutions.

It would therefore be unwise to end this book with anything more than a brief reminder of the main points that have been covered. However, the individual chapters have thrown up a number of common themes and these may sensibly be drawn together. Any summary of this sort is inevitably simplistic and cannot be comprehensive, but it may possibly be helpful as a checklist of the issues that have recurred most frequently in the individual chapters, and the points are therefore presented in that form.

The review of strategic development in Chapter 2 led us to three elements – focus, flexibility and future development – which were adopted as the stepping-off point for the main body of Chapters 3–7. Following that discussion, we can now consider a slightly longer list – for those who like catch phrases, 'the three Fs' can be replaced or complemented by 'the five Cs': concentration, customers, co-operation, competition and continuity.

Concentration

Concentration or focus on core competencies has been a major theme throughout this book. But the significance of concentration may also arise in other contexts, and it appears that in many cases firms may gain by concentrating resources to gain maximum leverage; by concentrating staff for project development into teams rather than separating them into functional ghettos; by concentrating procurements on to a limited number of trusted suppliers; and by concentrating or committing the resources needed to turn pioneering into long-term leadership. Clearly, concentration may appear as a major theme of strategic thinking.

Customers

Ultimately the success of a business depends neither on its resources nor on its products, but on its customers. It is the customers who sit at the end of the value chain as the ultimate arbiters of value; it is the customers who determine whether a new product will be successful; and it is the customers whose demands for quality and variety have often undermined strategies built on mass production and organisations built on hierarchical control. Strategists who ignore customers do so at their peril.

But customers, through brand loyalty, also enter the frame as one of the firm's resources. In particular, they may provide one of the key resources for diversification.

Co-operation

Co-operation through networks of relationships is a major feature of the context of business firms in Asia Pacific, and it has become increasingly important in Europe and America. Any strategic review should therefore consider the opportunities for co-operation, which might include the possibility of symbiosis between large and small firms; the use of co-operation to secure access to the resources needed for diversification or innovation; or the use of co-operation rather than vertical integration to secure the effective management of supply chains. Strategic alliances may be considered as a feasible alternative to merger for many strategic objectives, and may appear as the only feasible solution for mega-projects which require large, indivisible resources and involve high risk.

In general, both the characteristics of a firm and the choices which are open to it might be expected to include some reference to the impact of and opportunities for co-operation.

Competition

Co-operation may now extend into many areas of business but this does not make it a cosy community. Competition is still an essential aspect of the context in which a firm operates, and business strategy should be concerned to position the firm so as to make the best of its competitive strength and, if possible, to alter the rules of competition in its favour.

Aspects of competition have arisen in every chapter of this book. They include the relative assessment of strengths and weaknesses; the impact of consumer tastes and global competition; entry barriers and barriers to mobility; innovation and imitation; and competitive bidding for acquisitions. Competition is clearly an inescapable feature of strategy, but there are perhaps two overriding requirements. First, there is a need to watch all aspects of competition (suppliers, buyers, substitutes and new entrants) and not just existing competitors; and secondly, there is a fundamental need to understand the trade logic in every industry, market or niche in which the firm may operate.

Continuity

The final theme of this summary, continuity, applies both to the process and to the subject-matter of strategic analysis. A strategy is not a blueprint. It is concerned with objectives and positioning in the longer term but it cannot be fixed immutably. The context is always changing and as it changes it may be safer to look upon strategy as a continuous theme which is subject to continual review.

But continuity may also affect the choices themselves. Our review of the development of strategic thinking suggested that the consumers' search for continuous improvement is often reflected in the process of competition and in the role and nature of innovation; and may also have influenced the structure of many business organisations.

There are no rules for corporate strategy. In the absence of a rule-book these five Cs – concentration, customers, co-operation, competition and continuity – may serve as a checklist of the principal issues which have been raised in this book.

Bibliography

Abernethy, W. J. and Wayne, K. (1974) 'Limits of the Learning Curve', *Harvard Business Review*, 52, 109–19.

Acs, Z. J. and Audretsch, D. B. (1987) 'Innovation, Market Structure, and Firm Size', *Review of Economics and Statistics*, 69, 567–74.

Adelman, M. A. (1972) *The World Petroleum Market* (Baltimore, Johns Hopkins).

Amin, A. (1989) 'Flexible Specialisation and Small Firms in Italy: Myths and Realities', *Antipode*, 21, 13–34.

Baldwin, W. L. and Childs, G. L. (1969) 'The Fast Second and Rivalry in Research and Development', *Southern Economic Journal*, 36, 18–24.

Barney, J. B. (1988) 'Returns to Bidding Firms in Mergers and Acquisitions: Reconsidering the Relatedness Hypothesis', *Strategic Management Journal*, 9, 71–8.

Baumol, W. J. (1959) *Business Behaviour, Value and Growth* (New York, Macmillan).

Black, B. S. (1989) 'Bidder Overpayment in Takeovers', *Stanford Law Review*, 41, 597–659.

Blackhurst, C. (1996) 'What's It All About Stephen?', *Management Today*, February, 46–9.

Bolwijn, P. T. and Kumpe, T. (1990) 'Manufacturing in the 1990s – Productivity, Flexibility and Innovation', *Long Range Planning*, 23, 44–57.

Bowman, C. (1992) 'Interpreting Competitive Strategy', in Faulkner and Johnson (1992).

Buzzell, R. D. (1983) 'Is Vertical Integration Profitable?', *Harvard Business Review*, Jan/Feb, 92–102.

Buzzell, R. D. and Gale, B. T. (1987) *The PIMS Principles: Linking Strategy to Performance* (New York, Free Press).

Buzzell, R. D., Gale, B. T. and Sultan, R. G. M. (1975) 'Market Share – a Key to Profitability', *Harvard Business Review*, Jan/Feb, 97–106.

Cable, J. (ed.), (1994) *Current Issues in Industrial Economics* (London, Macmillan).

Caves, R. E. and Porter, M. (1977) 'From Entry Barriers to Mobility Barriers: Conjectural Decisions and the Contrived Deterrence to New Competition', *Quarterly Journal of Economics*, 34, 247–61.

CBI/NatWest (1997) *Innovation Trends Survey* (London, CBI and NatWest Innovation and Growth Unit).

Chandler, A. D. (1990a) *Scale and Scope: the Dynamics of Industrial Capitalism* (Cambridge Mass., Harvard University Press).

Chandler, A. D. (1990b) 'The Enduring Logic of Industrial Success', *Harvard Business Review*, March/April; reprinted in Montogomery and Porter (1991).

Channon, D. F. (1973) *The Strategy and Structure of British Enterprise* (London, Macmillan).

Christensen, C. R., Andrews, K. and Bower, J. (1965) *Business Policy: Text and Cases* (Burr Ridge, Irwin).

Clarke, R. (1985) *Industrial Economics* (Oxford, Blackwell).

Coase, R. H. (1937) 'The Nature of the Firm', *Economica*, 4, 386–405.

Collis, D. J. and Montgomery, C. A. (1997) *Corporate Strategy: Resources and the Scope of the Firm* (Chicago, Irwin).

Crainer, S. (1996) 'Not just a Game', *Management Today*, July, 66–8.
Cubbin, J. and Geroski, P. (1987) 'The Convergence of Profits in the Long Run: Inter-firm and Inter-industry Comparisons', *Journal of Industrial Economics*, 35, 427–42.
Cusumano, M. (1994) 'The Limits of Lean', *Sloan Management Review*, Summer, 27–32.
Drucker, P. F. (1987) *The Frontiers of Management* (London, Heinemann).
Dyas, G. P. and Thanheiser, H. T. (1976) *The Emerging European Enterprise: Strategy and Structure in French and German Industries* (quoted in Chandler, 1990a).
Edwards, R. S. and Townsend, H. (1962) *Business Enterprise* (London, Macmillan).
Ewing, D. E. (1958) *Long Range Planning for Management*. Quoted by R. N. Paul *et al.*, 'The Reality Gap in Strategic Planning', *Harvard Business Review*, 1978.
Faulkner, D. (1992) 'Strategic Alliances: Co-operation or Competition?', in Faulkner and Johnson (1992).
Faulkner, D. and Johnson, G. (1992) *The Challenge of Strategic Management* (London, Kogan Page).
Foster, R. N. (1986) *Innovation: The Attackers' Advantage* (London, Macmillan).
Gaughan, P. A. (1991) *Mergers and Acquisitions* (New York, HarperCollins).
Geroski, P. (1991) *Market Dynamics and Entry* (Oxford, Basil Blackwell).
Golder, P. N. and Tellis, G. J. (1993) 'Pioneering Advantage: Marketing Logic or Marketing Legend?', *Journal of Marketing Research*, 30, 158–70.
Gollop, F. and Monahan, J. (1991) 'A Generalized Index of Diversification: Trends in U.S. Manufacturing', *Review of Economics and Statistics*, 318–30.
Gorecki, P. K. (1975) 'An Inter-industry Analysis of Diversification in the UK Manufacturing Sector', *Journal of Industrial Economics*, 23, 131–46.
Gort, M. (1962) *Diversification and Integration in American Industry*, NBER General Series No. 77 (Princeton University Press).
Green, J. (1971) 'That Bureau Business', *Data Systems*, February, 19–35.
Green, S. and Berry, D. F. (1991) *Cultural, Structural and Strategic Change in Management Buyouts* (London, Macmillan).
Grossman, S. J. and Hart, O. D. (1986) 'The Costs and Benefits of Ownership: A Theory of Vertical and Lateral Integration', *Journal of Political Economy*, 94, 691–719.
Hamel, G. and Prahalad C. K. (1990) 'The Core Competence of the Organisation', *Harvard Business Review*, May/June; reprinted in Montgomery and Porter (1991).
Hamel, G. and Prahalad C. K. (1994) *Competing for the Future* (Harvard Business School Press).
Hammeresh, R. G. and Silk, S. B. (1979) 'How to Compete in Stagnant Industries', *Harvard Business Review*, Sept/Oct, 161–8.
Hansen, G. S. and Wernerfelt, B. (1989) 'Determinants of Firm Performance: The Relative Importance of Economic and Organisational Factors', *Strategic Management Journal*, 10, 399–411.
Haspeslagh, P. (1982) 'Portfolio Planning: Uses and Limits', *Harvard Business Review*, May/June, 64, 58–73.
Hatsopoulos, G. N. (1996) 'A Perpetual Idea Machine', *Daedalus (Journal of the American Academy of Arts and Science)*, 125, 81–94.
Heine, R. (1983) 'The Origins of Predictable Behaviour', *American Economic Review*, 73, 560–95.
Hill Samuel Bank Ltd (1989) *Mergers, Acquisitions and Alternative Corporate Strategies* (London, Mercury Books).

Hitt, M., Hoskisson, R. E., Johnson, R. A. and Moesel, D. D. (1996) 'The Market for Corporate Control and Firm Innovation', *Academy of Management Journal*, 39, 1084–119.

Hofstede, G. (1980) *Culture's Consequences: International Differences in Work-Related Values* (Beverly Hills, Sage).

Howe, W. S. (1986) *Corporate Strategy* (London, Macmillan).

Jensen, M. C. (1988) 'Takeovers: Their Causes and Consequences', *Journal of Economic Perspectives*, 2, 21–48.

Johnson, R. A. (1996) 'Antecedents and Outcomes of Corporate Refocusing', *Journal of Management*, 3, 439–83.

Karlof, B. (1989) *Business Strategy* (London, Macmillan).

Kester, W. C. (1991) *Japanese Takeovers: The Global Contest for Corporate Control* (Boston, Mass: Harvard Business School Press).

Lasserre, P. and Schütte, H. (1995) *Strategies for Asia Pacific* (London, Macmillan).

Leibenstein, H. (1996) 'Allocative Efficiency vs. X-Efficiency', *American Economic Review*, 56, 392–415.

Levitt, T. (1962) *Innovation in Marketing* (New York, McGraw-Hill).

Lewis, F. (1996) 'When the Bit Players Take Centre Stage', *Management Today*, March, 72–4.

Lorenz, A. (1995) 'BTR Breaks the Mould', *Management Today*, May, 45–9.

Lorenz, A. (1996) 'Unilever Changes Its Formula', *Management Today*, July, 44–8.

Lynn, M. (1996) 'Fortress Zeneca', *Management Today*, May, 72–6.

Mansfield, E. (1968) *Industrial Research and Technological Innovation* (New York, Norton).

Mansfield, E. and Wagner, S. (1975) 'Organisational and Strategic Factors Associated with the Probability of Success of Industrial R&D', *Journal of Business*, 48, 179–98.

Markides, C. C. (1993) 'Corporate Refocusing', *Business Strategy Review*, 4, 1–15.

Markides, C. C. (1995) 'Diversification, Restructuring and Economic Performance', *Strategic Management Journal*, 16, 101–18.

McGee, J. and Segal-Horn, S. (1990) 'Strategic Space and Industry Dynamics: The Implications for International Marketing Strategy', *Journal of Marketing Management*, 31, 175–93.

Mintzberg, H. (1987a) 'Crafting Strategy', *Harvard Business Review*, July/August.

Mintzberg, H. (1987b) 'Five Ps for Strategy', *California Management Review*, Fall.

Montgomery, C. A. and Porter, M. E. (1991) *Strategy: Seeking and Securing Competitive Advantage* (Harvard Business Review Book Series).

Morris, D. and Hergert, M. (1987) 'Trends in International Collaboration Agreements', *Columbia Journal of World Business*, Summer, 15–21.

Nonaka, I. (1991) 'The Knowledge-Creating Company', *Harvard Business Review*, November/December, 96–104.

Nooteboom, B. (1994) 'Innovation and Diffusion in Small Firms: Theory and Evidence', *Small Business Economics*, 6, 327–47.

North, D. C. (1990) *Institutions, Institutional Change and Economic Performance* (Cambridge, University Press).

Obolensky, N. (1994) *Practical Business Re-engineering* (London, Kogan Page).

Oliver, J. (1996) 'Superbaby Syndrome', *Management Today*, March, 54–8.

Penrose, E. T. (1959) *The Theory of the Growth of the Firm* (Oxford, Blackwell).

Peters, T. (1987) *Thriving on Chaos* (London, Macmillan).

Porter, M. E. (1979) 'How Competitive Forces Shape Strategy', *Harvard Business Review*, March/April; reprinted in Montogomery and Porter (1991).

Porter, M. E. (1980) *Competitive Strategy: Techniques for Analyzing Industries and Competitors* (New York, Free Press).

Porter ME, 1985, *Competitive Advantage* (New York, Free Press).

Pratten, C. F. (1971) *Economies of Scale in Manufacturing Industry* (Cambridge, University Press).

Pratten, C. F. (1991) *The Competitiveness of Small Firms* (Cambridge University Press).

Ravenscraft, D. and Scherer, F. M. (1987) *Mergers, Selloffs, and Economic Efficiency* (Washington, DC, Brookings Institution).

Rhys, D. G. (1972) *The Motor Industry* (London, Butterworth).

Rumelt, R. (1974) *Strategy, Structure and Economic Performance* (Cambridge, Mass., Harvard University Press).

Rumelt, R. (1991) 'How Much Does Industry Matter?', *Strategic Management Journal*, 12, 167–86.

Sadtler, D., Campbell, A. and Koch, R. (1997) *Break Up! When Large Companies Are Worth More Dead Than Alive* (Oxford, Capstone).

Saxenian, A. L. (1994) *Regional Advantage: Culture and Competition in Silicon Valley and Route 128* (Cambridge, Mass., Harvard University Press).

Scherer, F. M., Beckenstein, A., Kaufer, E., Murphy, D. R. and Bougeon-Massen, F. (1975) *The Economics of Multi-Plant Operation: An International Comparisons Study* (Cambridge, Mass., Harvard University Press).

Schmalensee, R. (1985) 'Do Markets Differ Much?', *American Economic Review*, 75, 341–51.

Schumpeter, J. (1928) 'The Instability of Capitalism', *Economic Journal*, 38, 361–86.

Scott, B. R. (1973) 'The Industrial State: Old Myths and New Realities', *Harvard Business Review*, March/April, 133–48.

Shaw, R. W. and Sutton, C. J. (1976) *Industry and Competition* (London, Macmillan).

Shleifer, A. and Vishney, W. (1991) 'Takeovers in the '60s and the '80s: Evidence and Implications', *Strategic Management Journal*, 12, 51–9.

Silberston, A. (1972) 'Economies of Scale in Theory and Practice', *Economic Journal*, supplement, 82, 369–91.

Singh, A. (1971) *Takeovers* (Cambridge University Press).

Singh, A. (1975) 'Takeovers, "Natural Selection", and the Theory of the Firm', *Economic Journal*, 85, 497–515.

Smith, D. (1996) 'Secrets of Hypergrowth', *Management Today*, February, 63–5.

Sutton, C. J. (1980) *Economics and Corporate Strategy* (Cambridge University Press).

Tellis, G. J. and Golder, P. N. (1996) 'First to Market, First to Fail? Real Causes of Enduring Market Leadership', *Sloan Management Review*, Winter, 65–75.

Thackray, J. (1995) 'That Vital Spark', *Management Today*, July, 56–8.

van de Vliet, A. (1996a) 'Walk Out and Start Up, *Management Today*, February, 50–2.

van de Vliet, A. (1996b) 'When the Haggling Has to Stop', *Management Today*, June, 56–60.

Vogel, H. L. (1994) *Entertainment Industry Economics*, 3rd edn (Cambridge University Press).

Walton, M. (1989) *The Deeming Management Method* (London, Mercury Books).

Webb, I. (1990) *Management Buyouts*, 2nd edn (Aldershot, Gower).

Wernerfelt, B. (1984) 'A Resource-based View of the Firm', *Strategic Management Journal*, 5, 171–80.

West, A. (1992) *Innovation Strategy* (Hemel Hempstead, Prentice-Hall).

Williamson, O. E. (1964) *The Economics of Discretionary Behaviour: Managerial Objectives in a Theory of the Firm* (Englewood Cliffs, NJ, Prentice-Hall).

Williamson, O. E. (1975) *Markets and Hierarchies* (New York, The Free Press).

Williamson, O. E. (1985) *The Economic Institutions of Capitalism* (New York, The Free Press).

Wind, Y. and Mahajan, V. (1988) 'Management Perspectives in Innovation', *Journal of Product Innovation Management*, 5, 270–84.

Index